First World War
and Army of Occupation
War Diary
France, Belgium and Germany

62 DIVISION
Divisional Troops
312 Brigade Royal Field Artillery
5 January 1917 - 31 August 1919

WO95/3075/2

The Naval & Military Press Ltd
www.nmarchive.com
Published in association with The National Archives

Published by

The Naval & Military Press Ltd

Unit 10 Ridgewood Industrial Park,

Uckfield, East Sussex,

TN22 5QE England

Tel: +44 (0) 1825 749494

www.naval-military-press.com

www.nmarchive.com

This diary has been reprinted in facsimile from the original. Any imperfections are inevitably reproduced and the quality may fall short of modern type and cartographic standards.

© **Crown Copyright**
Images reproduced by permission of The National Archives, London, England, 2015.

Contents

Document type	Place/Title	Date From	Date To
Heading	WO95/3075-2		
Heading	62nd Division 312th Brigade R.F.A. Jan 1917-1919 Aug		
Heading	War Diary 312 Brigade R.F.A. Original		
Heading	War Diary of 312c Bde R.F.A. From 5/1/17 To 1/2/17 Volume I		
War Diary	Northampton	05/01/1917	21/01/1917
War Diary	Occoches	23/01/1917	23/01/1917
War Diary	Amplier	23/01/1917	24/01/1917
War Diary	Louvencourt	25/01/1917	01/02/1917
Heading	War Diary 312 Brigade R.F.A. Volume II From 1st February To 28th February		
War Diary	Louvencourt	02/02/1917	11/02/1917
War Diary	Mailly Maillet	12/02/1917	28/02/1917
Heading	War Diary of 312 Brigade R.F.A. March 1917 Volume III		
War Diary	Station Road Beaucourt	01/03/1917	09/03/1917
War Diary	Miraumont	09/03/1917	25/03/1917
War Diary	Achiet-Le-Grand	26/03/1917	31/03/1917
Heading	War Diary of 312 Brigade R.F.A. From 1st April 1917 30th April 1917 Vol 4		
War Diary	Achiet-Le-Grand	02/04/1917	03/04/1917
War Diary	Ervillers	04/04/1917	09/04/1917
War Diary	Vraucourt	08/04/1917	25/04/1917
War Diary	Ecoust	26/04/1917	30/04/1917
Heading	War Diary of 312 Brigade R.F.A. May 1st To May 31st Vol 5		
War Diary	Ecoust	01/05/1917	15/05/1917
War Diary	Ecoust-St-Mein	15/05/1917	31/05/1917
Heading	War Diary of 312th Brigade R.F.A. Volume VI From 1st June 1917 To 30th June 1917		
War Diary	Ecoust-St-Mein	01/06/1917	30/06/1917
Heading	War Diary of 312th Brigade R.F.A. From 1st July 1917 To 31st July 1917 Vol VII		
War Diary		01/07/1917	31/07/1917
Heading	War Diary 312 Brigade R.F.A. From 1st August 1917 To 31st August 1917 Volume VIII		
War Diary	Lagnicourt	01/08/1917	31/08/1917
Heading	War Diary of 312th Brigade R.F.A. From 1st September 1917 To 30th September 1917 Volume IX		
War Diary		01/09/1917	30/09/1917
Heading	War Diary of 312th Brigade R.F.A. Volume X From 1st October 1917 To 31st October 1917		
War Diary		01/10/1917	31/10/1917
Heading	War Diary of 312th Brigade R.F.A. Volume XI From 1st November 1917 To 30th November 1917		
War Diary		01/11/1917	30/11/1917
Heading	War Diary of 312th Brigade R.F.A. Volume XII From 1st December 1917 To 31st December 1917		
War Diary		01/12/1917	31/12/1917

Heading	312 Brigade R.F.A. War Diary From 1st January 1918 To 31st January 1918 Volume XIII		
War Diary		01/01/1918	31/01/1918
Heading	312 Brigade R.F.A. War Diary From 1st Feb 1918 To 28th Feb 1918 Volume XIV		
War Diary	In The Field	01/02/1918	28/02/1918
Heading	62nd Divisional Artillery War Diary 312th Brigade R.F.A. March 1918		
Heading	War Diary 312th Brigade R.F.A. Vol XV		
War Diary		01/03/1918	31/03/1918
Heading	62nd Divisional Artillery War Diary 312th Brigade Royal Field Artillery April 1918		
Heading	War Diary of 312th Brigade R.F.A. From 1st April 1918 To 30th April 1918 Volume IV		
War Diary		01/04/1918	30/04/1918
Heading	312 Brigade R.F.A. War Diary From 1st May 1918 To 31st May 1918 Volume XVII		
War Diary		01/05/1918	31/05/1918
Heading	312 Brigade R.F.A. War Diary Volume XVIII From 1st June 1918 to 30th June 1918		
War Diary		01/06/1918	30/06/1918
Heading	Divl Artillery 62nd Division 312th Brigade R.F.A. July 1918		
War Diary	Orville	01/07/1918	16/07/1918
War Diary	Area of XXII Corps	17/07/1918	20/07/1918
War Diary	Ecueil Farm	20/07/1918	30/07/1918
War Diary	Aigny	31/07/1918	31/07/1918
Heading	War Diary of 312th Brigade R.F.A. Volume XX From 1st August 1918 To 31st August 1918		
War Diary	Chalons-Sur-Marne	01/08/1918	01/08/1918
War Diary	Bus (Les Artois)	02/08/1918	03/08/1918
War Diary	IV Corps	03/08/1918	15/08/1918
War Diary	57d N.E 1/20,000	16/08/1918	18/08/1918
War Diary	Essarts	19/08/1918	22/08/1918
War Diary	Puisieux Au-Mont 57d N.E	23/08/1918	23/08/1918
War Diary	Bertancourt	23/08/1918	23/08/1918
War Diary	Area of V Corps 57d N.E	24/08/1918	24/08/1918
War Diary	Pozieres	25/08/1918	26/08/1918
War Diary	57d S.E 1/20000	26/08/1918	26/08/1918
War Diary	High Wood 57c S.W 1/20,000	27/08/1918	28/08/1918
War Diary	Longueval Flers	29/08/1918	31/08/1918
Heading	312 Brigade R.F.A. War Diary From 1st September 1918 To 30th September 1918 Volume IX		
War Diary	Delville Wood	01/09/1918	01/09/1918
War Diary	III Army IV Corps Covering 38th Div	02/09/1918	02/09/1918
War Diary	Combles	02/09/1918	03/09/1918
War Diary	Mesnil-En-Arrouaise	04/09/1918	04/09/1918
War Diary	Mesnil Etricourt attd 21st Divn	05/09/1918	07/09/1918
War Diary	Courcelles	08/09/1918	08/09/1918
War Diary	VI Corps Beugny	09/09/1918	09/09/1918
War Diary	VI Corps 62nd Div Havrincourt	10/09/1918	14/09/1918
War Diary	Attd 3rd Div	15/09/1918	18/09/1918
War Diary	Havrincourt VI Corps 3rd Div	19/09/1918	27/09/1918
War Diary	Ribecourt	28/09/1918	29/09/1918
War Diary	Marcoing	30/09/1918	30/09/1918

Heading	War Diary 312 Brigade R.F.A. From 1st October 1918 To 31st October 1918 Volume XXII		
War Diary	Marcoing VI Corps 62nd D.A (Sherlock Group)	01/10/1918	02/10/1918
War Diary	3rd D.A (Sherlock Group)	03/10/1918	05/10/1918
War Diary	Marcoing 3rd D.A (Mair Group)	06/10/1918	06/10/1918
War Diary	Marcoing VI Corps 3rd D.A.	07/10/1918	07/10/1918
War Diary	Rumilly	08/10/1918	08/10/1918
War Diary	Guards D.A	09/10/1918	09/10/1918
War Diary	Seranvillers	09/10/1918	09/10/1918
War Diary	Cattenieres Estourmel Guards D.A.	10/10/1918	10/10/1918
War Diary	62nd D.A	11/10/1918	15/10/1918
War Diary	Quievy Guards D.A 62nd D.A	16/10/1918	20/10/1918
War Diary	Quievy-Solesmes 62nd D.A.	20/10/1918	20/10/1918
War Diary	St Python	21/10/1918	21/10/1918
War Diary	Solesmes	22/10/1918	22/10/1918
War Diary	3rd D.A	23/10/1918	23/10/1918
War Diary	Vertain 3rd D.A	23/10/1918	23/10/1918
War Diary	Escarmain	24/10/1918	25/10/1918
War Diary	62nd D.A	26/10/1918	31/10/1918
Miscellaneous	Appendix A	23/10/1918	23/10/1918
Heading	War Diary 312th Brigade R.F.A. November Volume XXIII		
War Diary	Quievy	01/11/1918	02/11/1918
War Diary	Vertain	03/11/1918	03/11/1918
War Diary	Ruesnes	03/11/1918	04/11/1918
War Diary	Bellevue Fm	04/11/1918	04/11/1918
War Diary	La Belle Maison	04/11/1918	04/11/1918
War Diary	R.12.b.8.3	05/11/1918	05/11/1918
War Diary	L'Orgnies Area	05/11/1918	05/11/1918
War Diary	Gommegnies	05/11/1918	06/11/1918
War Diary	Le Cavee N.7.c.6.2	06/11/1918	06/11/1918
War Diary	Le Cavee N.7.c.6.3	07/11/1918	07/11/1918
War Diary	Le Timon	08/11/1918	08/11/1918
War Diary	P.14.c.2.6	08/11/1918	08/11/1918
War Diary	P.14.c.2.6 Tri-Mouton Area	09/11/1918	09/11/1918
War Diary	Sous-Le-Bois Q.7	10/11/1918	18/11/1918
War Diary	Ferriere Le Grand A.3	19/11/1918	19/11/1918
War Diary	Hantes Wiheries C.3	20/11/1918	20/11/1918
War Diary	Thy-Le-Chateau F.3	21/11/1918	24/11/1918
War Diary	Gerpinnes G.2	25/11/1918	25/11/1918
War Diary	Furnaux I.3	26/11/1918	26/11/1918
War Diary	Maredret J.3	27/11/1918	27/11/1918
War Diary	Thynes L.3	28/11/1918	30/11/1918
Heading	War Diary December 1918 312th Brigade R.F.A. Volume XXIV		
War Diary	Thynes L.3	01/12/1918	10/12/1918
War Diary	Ychippe B.3	11/12/1918	11/12/1918
War Diary	Barvaux Condroz	12/12/1918	12/12/1918
War Diary	Borlon E.2	13/12/1918	13/12/1918
War Diary	Jehoge H.1	14/12/1918	14/12/1918
War Diary	Chevron I.2	15/12/1918	16/12/1918
War Diary	Trois Ponts	17/12/1918	17/12/1918
War Diary	Okdenval I.M E.3	18/12/1918	18/12/1918
War Diary	Okdenval E.3	19/12/1918	20/12/1918
War Diary	Okdenval I.M E.3	21/12/1918	21/12/1918
War Diary	Lager Elsenborn I.M F.1	22/12/1918	22/12/1918

War Diary	Hofen I.L G.11	23/12/1918	23/12/1918
War Diary	Wollseifen I.L I.10	24/12/1918	25/12/1918
War Diary	Gemund I.L	26/12/1918	31/12/1918
Heading	War Diary 312th Brigade R.F.A. January 1919 Vol 25		
War Diary	Gemund	01/01/1919	31/01/1919
Heading	War Diary 312th Brigade R.F.A. February 1919 Vol 26		
War Diary	Gemund	01/02/1919	27/02/1919
Heading	March 312th Brigade R.F.A. War Diary 1-3-19-31-3-19 Volume XVII		
War Diary	Gemund Germany	01/03/1919	31/03/1919
Heading	War Diary 312th Bde R.F.A. May 1919		
War Diary	Gemund	00/05/1919	00/05/1919
Heading	War Diary 312th Bde R.F.A. June 1919		
War Diary	Gemund	12/06/1919	12/06/1919
Heading	War Diary 312th Bde R.F.A. July 1919		
War Diary	Gemund	00/07/1919	00/07/1919
Heading	312 Brigade R.F.A. War Diary August 1919		
War Diary	Gemund Germany	01/08/1919	16/08/1919
War Diary	Heytesbury Camp Wiltshire	17/08/1919	31/08/1919

work 2075 (2)

62ND DIVISION

312TH BRIGADE R.F.A.

JAN 1917 - ~~DEC 1918~~ 1919 AUG

62ND DIVISION

WAR DIARY

312 Brigade RFA

Original

Vol I

ORIGINAL

WAR DIARY
OF
312 C/Bde R.F.A.
from 5/1/17 to 1/2/17.
Volume I.

SECRET.

Army Form C. 2118.

Instructions regarding War Diaries and Intelligence Summaries are contained in F.S. Regs., Part II. and the Staff Manual respectively. Title pages will be prepared in manuscript.

WAR DIARY or 312 Brigade RFA
INTELLIGENCE SUMMARY.
(Erase heading not required.)

Place	Date	Hour	Summary of Events and Information	Remarks and references to Appendices
Northampton	5/1/17	2 am	Brigade commenced to leave Northampton en route for Southampton, and cleared by noon. A + C Batteries sailed from Southampton in boat E 5021 and B Battery in "North Western Miller". BD/Battery + Medium Trench Mortar Battery sailed by boat "Biper" and other ½ D/Battery and H.Q. Staff in boat "Siptah". The Brigade disembarked at LE HAVRE and spent one day in Rest Camps as follows :— A.B. +C. Batteries in Docks Rest Camp.	
	6/1/17		D/Battery and H.Q. Staff at No 2 Rest Camp, Harfleur. The journey was continued on the afternoon and evening of the 6th inst and the Brigade detrained at AUXI-LE-CHATEAU and marched to Rest Billets at OCCOCHES.	
	7/1/17		Arranged of Billets. Batteries occupying barns and H.Q. Staff at the CHATEAU. Heavy Trench Mortar Battery attached to D/Battery and Heavy Trench Mortar Battery temporarily attached to A.B. +C. Batteries. Weather wet and roads and district in very muddy conditions.	
	9/1/17	9.30am	Heavy Trench Mortar Battery rejoined 310 Brigade RFA	
	14/1/17	10am	Inspection of Billets by G.O.C 62nd Division	
	15/1/17		Death of 3 horses reported to 340th RA 62nd Division. C Battery lost one horse reported 17/1/17	
	17/1/17	10.30am	Party consisting of 2 Officers and 340 Other Ranks for Battery and 1 Officer and 8 Other Ranks H.Q. Staff left OCCOCHES for a period of instruction with 19th D.A. at COIGNEUX	
	18/1/17	12.10pm	1 Officer and 48 O. Ranks reported arrival from D/311 Brigade RFA + 58 horses D/313 Battery reorganized to 6 Guns + 5" QF Howitzers under command of Major F H LISTER. D.S.O. RA	
	19/1/-		Routine work in billets. Operation Order No 1. received	
	20/1/-			

Army Form C. 2118

WAR DIARY
of 312 Brigade RFA
INTELLIGENCE SUMMARY
(Erase heading not required.)

Instructions regarding War Diaries and Intelligence Summaries are contained in F.S. Regs., Part II. and the Staff Manual respectively. Title Pages will be prepared in manuscript.

Place	Date	Hour	Summary of Events and Information	Remarks and references to Appendices
Occoches	23/1/17	11.30 am	Brigade left OCCOCHES. Weather very frosty but dry. HQrs leading column followed by Batteries in rotation. Route - via DOULENS to AMPLIER. Arrived at AMPLIER 1.30pm. Horses billeted on road sides and gun parks in market square and in fields around village. Weather continued dry but very frosty.	
Amplier	23/1/17 & 24/1/17	10.15 am	Brigade left AMPLIER at 10.15 am. A/312 Battery leading. HQrs bringing up rear. Journey was broken by many halts. Brigade arrived LOUVENCOURT at 3pm. No accommodation in town. Horses picketed in open fields. Men in tents. Weather dry & very frosty. Watering facilities very bad.	
Louvencourt	25/1/17		Routine work. 16 offrs & frost.	
	26/1/17	9.30 am	Party of 1 Corpl + 7 Gunners joined Brigade from 310 Brigade RFA. Routine work	
	27/1/17	9.30 am	Party of 1 Bombardier, 1 Saddler + 13 drivers sunplies to establish horse transport to hold BAC at THIEVRES for 311 Brigade BAC	
		1 pm	Twelve party of 9 Officers + 96 Other ranks attached to 10th Brigade for training. First party returned	
	30/1/17	10 pm	Relief Orders & Instructions received	
	31/1/17		Lt Colonel Bedwell proceeded to 35th Brigade RFA and inspected all Battery positions in preparation for relief Batteries to take over from 35th Bde RFA on the nights of 5th & 6th February	
	1/2/17	noon	and 7/8 February. Joined to take over on the 7/8 February. Party of 9 Officers and 96 Other Ranks returned to Brigade	

E.M. Bedwell
LIEUT. COL. : R.F.A.
COMMDG. 312th BRIGADE ROYAL FIELD ARTILLERY.

Original

Vol 2

War Diary
312 Brigade, R.F.A.

Volume 14

From 1st February
To 28th February

WAR DIARY
INTELLIGENCE SUMMARY

of 312 Brigade Royal Field Artillery

Army Form C. 2118

Month: February

Place	Date	Hour	Summary of Events and Information	Remarks and references to Appendices
Louvencourt	2/2/17		Routine Work. Weather still very good & frosty. Capt Bryan took over command of B/312 Battery from Gallimore, who went to B/Battery as Captain. Lieut Sutherland transferred from D & B Battery.	
	3/2/17		Routine Work. No change in weather. Lieut G. Addison posted to C/310 Battery as Capt.	
	4/2/17		Colonel proceeded up line to inspect new positions. Weather frosty.	
	5/2/17		Lieut C Hardy C/312 Battery attached to No 15 Squadron RFC for instruction in Cooperation between Artillery & Flying Corps - 14 days course. Routine work.	
			Relief of Divnl Arty did not commence as ordered.	
	6/2/17	6 pm	Lieut Thompson transferred from B/311 Battery RFA posted to A/312 Battery RFA.	
	8/2/17	2 pm	Lieut COINNES and party proceeded to VAUCHELLES to French Mortar School for course of firing. Billeted at BELLEGLISE. Routine work. Cottages & 200 men accommodated in tents.	
			Still to allow Infantry to come in 200 men accommodated in tents.	
	9/2/17		Instructions for Relief No 3 received.	
	10/2/17	9 am	Colonel with Adjutant & OC & Battery Commanders proceeded to view positions. Colonel, Adjutant proceeded to MAILLY MAILLET to prepare to take over. One detachment.	
	11/2/17	10.30 am	Colonel, Adjutant proceeded to MAILLY MAILLET to prepare to take over. One detachment per Battery took over from Bathurst in action.	
Mailly Maillet	12/2/17		Batteries took over from LOUVENCOURT to MAILLY MAILLET and occupied billets at Headquarters Staff marched from LOUVENCOURT to MAILLY MAILLET Remainder of Batteries marched to MAILLY MAILLET from HQ. 312 Brigade RFA. LOUVENCOURT and took over as under. A/312 Took over 12th Battery RFA B/312 " " 25th " " C/312 " " 5th " " D/312 " " 3/01 " "	

Army Form C. 2118

WAR DIARY
or
INTELLIGENCE SUMMARY

of 312 Brigade RFA

Sheet 2

(Erase heading not required.)

Instructions regarding War Diaries and Intelligence Summaries are contained in F.S. Regs., Part II. and the Staff Manual respectively. Title Pages will be prepared in manuscript.

Place	Date	Hour	Summary of Events and Information	Remarks and references to Appendices
MAILLY MAILLET	13/2/17	6am	Routine fire and registration of guns carried out during day. S.O.S. Barrage and protective barrage.	
	14/2/17	6am	Routine fire and registration of guns carried out. Enemy shelled very heavily from 30 cm to mm with 77mm + 150mm + 105mm guns. Battery observed by F.L.O at K30.a.21 (Sheet 57 D NE) and fire opened on her with 100 yards radius of point. S.O.C. Barrage fire has now but then normal night fire/track returned.	
		6pm		
	15/2/17		Registration carried on K.36.B (Sheet 57 D NE) and PENDANT COPSE. Enemy shelled in vicinity of AUCHONVILLERS and WALKER ALLEY all day.	
	16/2/17	9am to 4pm	Routine firing on K.36.B (Sheet 57 D NE) and PENDANT COPSE. Enemy shelled in vicinity of AUCHONVILLERS and WALKER ALLEY all day.	
		5.20pm	Guns 5&9 shells dropped on C/Battery position and others dropped on A/Battery. Enemy aeroplanes observed. Enemy aeroplane at Q15.b.40.55 (Sheet 57 D NE) fired on A/Battery position until driven off by Lewis anti-aircraft gun fire. Visibility was very poor all day.	
	16/2/17	6pm to 12 mdnt	18 rounds task allotted to B/Battery 10 rounds per hour on road junction NORTH of TEN TREE ALLEY K.36.c.67 (Sheet 57 D NE)	
	17/2/17	5.10	S.O.S. Barrage placed until 6.15am. Enemy shelled heavily during night. Visibility very bad. Enemy machine gun located at K36.a.87 (Sheet 57 D NE) and guns round at K36.a.87 were fired on by us 30 rounds 4.5" Howitzer. Enemy's fire and our own very quiet all day and night.	
	18/2/17		Intermittent firing on PENDANT ALLEY/EAST, WING TRENCH + PENDANT TRENCH around NICHONVILLERS. Recently sunk 4.5" + 5.9" Howitzer. A/Battery fired off 4 on clinic the day on suspected Machine gun emplacement at K.36.a.8.9. Enemy shelled intermittently all night.	
	19/2/17		Battery day + night tasks. Retaliation on PENDANT COPSE at 4pm 50 rnds by D/Battery, Retaliation & recent fire on PENDANT COPSE at 6pm 50 rnds by E/Battery. A/Battery fired on machine gun emplacements at K36.a.8.9 + L.31.B.14 (Sheet 57 D NE). Enemy shelled intermittently all day. Enfilade at K36.a.8.9 + L.31.B.14 (Sheet 57 D NE).	

1875 Wt. W.593/326 1,000,000 4/15 J.B.C. & A. A.D.S.S./Forms/C. 2118.

Army Form C. 2118

Instructions regarding War Diaries and Intelligence Summaries are contained in F.S. Regs., Part II. and the Staff Manual respectively. Title Pages will be prepared in manuscript.

WAR DIARY
~~INTELLIGENCE SUMMARY~~ of 312 Brigade RFA Sheet 3

(Erase heading not required.)

Place	Date	Hour	Summary of Events and Information	Remarks and references to Appendices
MAILLY MAILLET	19/2/17		Major Evans and Capt Callinan observing at KYLE POST noticed the enemy were shelling our posts S of TEN TREE ALLEY with hi[gh]v gun (calibre approx) 3 red rockets were sent up apparently from posts in TEN TREE ALLEY when enemy lengthened range and switched to right, then two red rockets were sent up and the enemy further lengthened range and switched to the right. Our one red rocket sent the enemy Kelv[?] range and lines. Weather dull. Wind N'ly Wind S.S.E.	
	20/2/17		Ordinary day & night tasks. Enemy shelled our OP at GOUGH POST heavily. A Battery fired a machine gun emplacement at K.36.a.8.7. The Colonel observed that the guns shelling WAGON ROAD 2 days ago seem to have been shifted as the road is now being extensively enfiladed by guns probably in SERRE or N O'SERRE.	
	21/2/17	4.40 pm	Firing on junction of trenches around L.36.c.4.6 and L.35.c.5.5. Bursts of fire on WING TRENCH. Swing on TENDANT ALLEY W. Nightfiring on POMPOM & RUSH ALLEYS. OP at GOUGH POST heavily shelled by 5.9" guns from direction of PUISIEUX. Machine guns fired on at K.36.a.8.7. L.31.a.9.4 and L.K.36.L.5.8 (Shell 57d NE)	
	22/2/17		Morning day & night firing on TENDANT COPSE, WING TRENCH + around L.26.c.4. G.25.C.9.2. OP at GOUGH POST heavily shelled for 2 hours from 2pm to 4.40pm from direction of MIRAUMONT. 50 rounds fired by A Battery at Suspected machine gun at K.36.b.5.8.	
	23/2/17		Ordinary day & night tasks. A Battery new position recently shelled by 5.9" shrapnel. At 2pm. Registration on TENDANT COPSE carried out by A. C. + D. Batteries by the Sec. turn to new positions.	
	11/2/17		Lieut KENSETT joined from 340 Brigade RFA and posted to C/312 Battery RFA. Returned wounded N of Gommecourt in V Corps front. Lt. Col B [?] seconded to Army [?]	
	24/2/17		command of Left Group.	
		5.30pm 11.45pm	NOT CHECKED FOR ERRORS issued by Left Group Commander Enemy [?] to proceed to MAILLY and relieve officers	

1875 Wt. W593/826 1,000,000 4/15 J.B.C.& A. A.D.S.S./Forms/C. 2118.

WAR DIARY

312 Brigade RA

INTELLIGENCE SUMMARY

Army Form C. 2118.

Sheet 1

Place	Date	Hour	Summary of Events and Information	Remarks and references to Appendices
MAILLY				
MAILLY	24/2/17	11.45pm	to be in readiness for early move	
		5pm	Enemy further retired. Brigade stood to awaiting orders to move up following the retirement. No firing was done all day owing to uncertainty of our Infantry patrol movements. Batteries reconnoitre published gun positions in Wagon Road.	
	26/2/17	10am	Orders received for Major Swan to reconnoitre positions in BEAU REGARD DOVECOTE and to get his Battery into action at night. 18pdr Batteries reconnoitred positions in BOIS D'HOLLANDE, and Colonel worked advanced posh Adjutant rode to STATION ROAD beyond BEAUMONT HAMEL and marked Brigade HQrs.	
		8pm	B/312 in action	
	27/2/17	8am	Brigade HQrs left MAILLY and marched to STATION ROAD with wagon lines at AUCHONVILLERS. A+C batteries marched up into new positions.	
	28/2/17		Owing to bad visibility registration could not be carried out very well.	

28/2/17

J.W.M. [signature] Lt Col
Cmdg 312 Bde RA

Vol 3

War Diary
of
312 Brigade RFA.
March 1917

VOLUME III

Original.

ORIGINAL

Army Form C. 2118.

WAR DIARY
of 3rd Brigade RFA
INTELLIGENCE SUMMARY.
(Erase heading not required.)

1st Sheet

Place	Date	Hour	Summary of Events and Information	Remarks and references to Appendices
STATION ROAD BEAUCOURT	1/3/17		Registration carried out. S.O.S. from 12.30 a.m. to 12.35 a.m. Enemy observation balloons and aeroplanes seen during the day. 11 Aeroplanes over our lines	
	2/3/17		Visibility good all day. R.S.a.35 Visibility poor. B/Battery moved up to new position beyond Miraumont 3 guns in position by night. Enemy shelled heavily with 5.9's & gas shells. Following officers joined and posted as follows:- Lieut R.C. FURLONG posted to A/312 Battery RFA Lieut V. St G KNAGGS -do- B/312 -do- Lieut H.H LAWRENCE -do- C/312 -do- Lieut E.S LLOYD -do- D/312 -do-	
	3/3/17		B/Battery moved forward to new position at MIRAUMONT in R.S.a.27. Positions were shelled heavily during the day by heavy guns of the enemy. HQ. Staff position reconnoitred and party sent up to occupy. A & C Batteries reconnoitred new positions and parties working on gun positions. 2/Lt. E.P BEDNELL R.A evacuated	
	10 am		sick and admitted to hospital. 2/Lt Col F.E.L.BARKER took over temporary command of the Brigade in absence of its commander. Ammunition sent up to Batteries HQ.	

ORIGINAL

Army Form C. 2118.

WAR DIARY
of 312 Brigade RFA

~~INTELLIGENCE~~ SUMMARY.

(Erase heading not required.)

One Sheet

Instructions regarding War Diaries and Intelligence Summaries are contained in F. S. Regs., Part II. and the Staff Manual respectively. Title pages will be prepared in manuscript.

Place	Date	Hour	Summary of Events and Information	Remarks and references to Appendices
STATION ROAD BEAUCOURT	3/3/17		by pack horses. B/Battery reported casualty to one other rank.	
	4/3/17	4am	A & C Batteries moved up to forward positions. B Battery position now occupied by Jack horses. A = L.34.c.1.7 B = R5a.27 C = L.33.b.55 D = R5a.35 ('/10000 MAP ACHIET 5a) A = Sgd 10 – Sgd 0.7 Batteries engaged in wire cutting	
	5/3/17	5am	B/Battery Howitzer No 869 knocked by direct hit. no casualties. Wire cutting impossible owing to poor visibility. Batteries consolidating positions.	
		9pm	Orders re night attack received from G + E.	
	6/3/17	12.30am	B/Battery shelled area around ACHIET. B - PETIT to prevent stragglers getting away. Wire cutting programme continued around ACHIET. 6 - PETIT. Lieut SPARLING and Lieut EDWARD reported arrival & posted to C & B batteries respectively.	
	7/3/17			
	8/3/17 2pm		H.Q. Staff moved forward into R4-c-chal. Killed nearly all afternoon. Instructions No 4 received and 2/Col FRL BARKER took over command of Left Group. From 1-30pm – 1-50pm 18 John Batteries Sprinkled approaches to ACHIET - 6 - PETIT. Rate of fire 1 round per gun per minute. Instructions NO 5 received. During day wire cutting carried out by R/Bn	
	9/3/17		Batteries with good effects. A/Battery warned to enfilade ditch G.19 – G.20.	

WAR DIARY
of 312 Brigade RFA
INTELLIGENCE SUMMARY
(Erase heading not required.)

Army Form C. 2118.

Remarks and references to Appendices: **3a Sheet**

Place	Date	Hour	Summary of Events and Information
MIRAUMONT	9/3/17		2nd & guns of D/Battery to shell STEP TRENCH G.20.a.25 – G.19.a.2.3. This
	10/3/17	5.15a	bombardment was duly commenced at 5.15am 10/3/17 at intervals of gunfire for 2 minutes During day batteries fired occasional bursts on DITCH in G.19 and G.20 in aid of II Corps. At 6.20am Major Scott captured 2nd & German Prisoners
surrendered to D/312 Bty		6.20a	went handed over to 187th Brigade. Lieut. COMPTON reported arrival + posted to B/312 Battery RFA.
	11/3/17		Wire cutting tasks carried on as follows C/Battery L.24.a.9½.1 to L.24.a.9.2½. B/Battery G.19.a.0.8 – G.19.a.0.9. A/Battery G.19.a.0.9 – L.24.a.9.½.1. Wire cutting stopped during storm – 14th RFA Brigade joined Left
		6p	Group and communication opened. HQ Staff in R & central heavily shelled with 8 inch howitzers. Wire cutting continued but visibility too poor to observe damage done.
	12/3/17	9.55p	BM 19 received and Batteries warned to double usual amount of ammn on approaches to ACHIET-le-PETIT.
	13/3/17		No wire cutting carried out owing to poor visibility. Fired on suspected H.gun machine gun emplacement 3 rounds by D/Battery. During night Batteries

OC 2 GWA/2

Army Form C. 2118.

WAR DIARY
of 32 Brigade RFA

INTELLIGENCE SUMMARY.
(Erase heading not required.)

Place	Date	Hour	Summary of Events and Information	Remarks and references to Appendices
MIRAUMONT	13/3/17		Fired on back approaches to ACHIET-Le-PETIT Battery positions heavily shelled by 5.9" Howr from 8pm to 9-10pm Lachrymatory shells dropped around Battery positions and a few 8" HV shells on railway in front of HQ position	
	14/3/17		No wire cutting carried out owing to hazy paths being on. At 8.30pm commenced firing again on cross roads to rear of ACHIET-Le-PETIT. This was stopped again at 5 to 8.30pm owing to infantry patrols being out.	
	15/3/17	6.30am	On 15/3/17 owing to reported further retirement of Germans at BIHUCOURT Morning cutting done all day. Fired on cross roads to rear of ACHIET-Le-PETIT and B/Battery fired on trench when Germans observed to be moving about. OC C/A Battery reconnoitred suitable new positions near ACHIET.	
	16/3/17		B/Battery fired 36 rounds on wire in front of ACHIET-Le-PETIT but owing to heavy mist result could not be observed. Orders received for Brigade to hold itself in readiness to move at 4 hours notice. Reconnaissance of ACHIET carried out.	
	17/3/17		No wire cutting done. On section of A/Battery to hold itself in readiness to move forward with Infantry as advance guard.	
	18/3/17		Brigade stood to awaiting orders to move. Batteries engaged in collecting stores	
	19/3/17		Germans to Brigade Dumps A+C Batteries at L34 b.1.3 BHQ at R5 a.1.6	

T2134. Wt. W708—776. 500000. 4/15. Sir J. C. & S.

Army Form C. 2118.

6721 9/1/12

WAR DIARY
of 32 Brigade RFA
S. L. Shell

INTELLIGENCE SUMMARY.
(Erase heading not required.)

Place	Date	Hour	Summary of Events and Information	Remarks and references to Appendices
MIRAUMONT	20/3/17		Brigade Shelled in old positions. Wagon lines moved up to BOIS D'HOLLANDE + hour moved to Northern portions. Further ammon dumped. D/76 Battery ordered to be ready to move at dawn followed by A + C Batteries.	
	21/3/17		B/ Battery moved to GOMMECOURT A + C Batteries also moved to ERVILLERS as part of advanced guard and came under orders of Colonel MARTURN G.O.C 2 Division Advance Guard. Batteries in action 21/3/1917 as follow	
			A/ Battery 6 guns in action at B2 d 87.	
			— " — 2 " resting at MIRAUMONT	
			B/ Battery 6 " " " " "	
			C/ Battery 4 " in action . B9.c.4.2	
			D/ Battery 6 " " " " "	
	22/3/17		Lieut C.N POLLAN Killed in action	
		9.30 am	Lieut Col E.P. BEDNELL rejoined from No 1 Red Cross Hospital and Lieut Col F.E.L BARKER relinquished command of Brigade. One 18 pdr gun 2 ammon wagons 176 rounds ammon 2 Officers 11 Other Ranks and 2 horses proceeded from B/ Battery to S.9 central with 310 Brigade RFA	

ORIGINAL

Army Form C. 2118.

WAR DIARY
of 32 Brigade RFA
INTELLIGENCE SUMMARY
(Erase heading not required.)

6th Sheet

Instructions regarding War Diaries and Intelligence Summaries are contained in F. S. Regs., Part II. and the Staff Manual respectively. Title pages will be prepared in manuscript.

Place	Date	Hour	Summary of Events and Information	Remarks and references to Appendices
MIRAUMONT	23/3/17		of B/Battery — One gun and two ammunition wagons proceeded to G.9 central.	
	24/3/17		One gun and two further ammunition wagons of B/Battery proceeded to G.9 central.	
	25/3/17		Major D.S.H. WOODWARD posted to A/310 Brigade RFA. Lt. Col. F.P. BEDWELL proceeded to ACHIET-le-GRAND and selected quarters for HQ Staff at G.10.a.6.2. and during the day one gun + two ammn wagons of B/Battery proceeded to G.9 central.	
	25/3/17		Lieut N.T. ASTLEY and advance party proceeded to ACHIET-le-GRAND to prepare billet. One gun and two ammn wagons of B/Battery proceeded to G.9 central.	
ACHIET-le-GRAND	26/3/17	11am	Brigade Headquarters left MIRAUMONT and proceeded to ACHIET-le-GRAND.	
	27/3/17		One gun and two wagons of B/Battery moved from MIRAUMONT. All battery now at ACHIET-le-GRAND.	
	28/3/17		Brigade HQ Staff engaged in clearing and billets. Sticks of dynamite found in quantity and destroyed.	
	29/30/3/17		Clearing of billets & routine work.	
	31/3/17		2nd Lt. W. WULSCROFT posted to A/312. 2nd Lt. F.C. BALL posted to A/312 — Lieut. J.A. BROWN posted to D/312 and Lt. Col. WIGGS refunded arrival and attached to HQ Staff.	

WAR DIARY
of 312 Brigade RFA

INTELLIGENCE SUMMARY
(Erase heading not required.)

Army Form C. 2118.

Place	Date	Hour	Summary of Events and Information	Remarks and references to Appendices
ACHIET-LE-GRAND	31/3/17		Reported to Headquarters RFA 62nd Division - Batteries of 312 Brigade RFA in action as follows: A at T.27.b.5.0 B at B.9.a.2½.1 C at B.24.d.3.7½ D at T.27.d.3.2	

Secret.

Vol 4

War Diary
of
31² Brigade RFA

ORIGINAL COPY.

Volume IV

From 1st April 1917
30th April 1917

ORIGINAL

Army Form C. 2118.

WAR DIARY
of 3/2 Brigade R.F.A.
INTELLIGENCE SUMMARY
(Erase heading not required.)

Sheet 1.

Place	Date	Hour	Summary of Events and Information	Remarks and references to Appendices
ACHIET-LE-GRAND	2/4/17	5.30am	Batteries under 7th Divisional Arty. helped in attack on CROISELLES with sweeping barrage fire, which was entirely successful. Recd N.T.ASTLEY proceeded to ERVILLERS to find billets for Brigade HQrs.	
ERVILLERS	3/4/17		H.Q. Staff moved to No.3 Billet ERVILLERS. One section of batteries moved to ECOUST. 62nd D.A. Instruction No.19 copy No.2 received. 2/Lt.P.BEDWELL took up Liaison Office of 185th Infantry Brigade Headquarters BIHUCOURT. B/312. 2.32	
	4/4/17 5/4/17		proceeded to No.Ry. to allow HQrs for Brigade B/312 sustained heavy casualties to forward section. 62nd Divisional Instruction No.20 Copy No.2 received. C/312 Battery attached to A/Group. B/312 Battery attached to B/Group. A/312 + D/312 Battery attached to D/Group.	
	6/4/17		Advance party of H.Q.Staff proceeded to Bn-058. H.Q.Staff opened there. Communication established with Batteries. Latter engaged in cutting wire around BULLECOURT. New scheme at 10-2 p.m. ERVILLERS causing casualties to D/Battery. Remainder of H.Q.Staff moved to Bn-058.	
	7/4/17 9/4/17		Dr. Ellis & Gnr. Kerry D/Battery awarded Military Medal for conspicuous bravery	Stbd

ORIGINAL

Army Form C. 2118.

WAR DIARY
of 312 Brigade RFA
INTELLIGENCE SUMMARY
(Erase heading not required.)

Incl Sheet

Place	Date	Hour	Summary of Events and Information	Remarks and references to Appendices
VRUCOURT	8/4/17		Batteries engaged in wirecutting during morning from 3 pm – 3.10 pm Batteries bombarded enemy's front - wire Own frontage as for wirecutting. Rate of fire 2 rounds per gun per minute. No firing carried out from 12 midnight – 3 am – 9/4/17.	
	9/4/17		Bombardment of enemy's front from 5.30 am Rate of fire 2 rounds per gun per minute at 11.30 am further bombardment carried out of enemy's front. Opened fire 11.30 am on same front as for wirecutting - at 11.33 am lift on to enemy's front line trench - 11.36 am lift 100 yards 11.39 am lift to enemy's Second line trench + cease fire at 11.40 am. This was carried out by Batteries during remainds of day wire cutting carried out wire cutting. Batteries Shelled heavily all day. Batteries ceased fire from 8.10 pm – 10.15 pm.	
	10/4/17		Batteries were ready to move at short notice. Bombardment of enemy's front line + support trenches carried out at 4-30 am. During day very quiet but wire cutting commenced again during afternoon.	
	11/4/17	4.30 am	A further bombardment of the enemy front carried at Wayne Farm moved up to vicinity of Ruyaulcourt HQrs. Bty but owing to action not	Stef

ORIGINAL

Army Form C. 2118.

WAR DIARY

of 312 Brigade RFA Sadler

~~INTELLIGENCE~~ SUMMARY.

(Erase heading not required.)

Place	Date	Hour	Summary of Events and Information	Remarks and references to Appendices
VRAUCOURT	11/4/17 12/4/17		Nothing Since they returned to STRILLERS. No wirecutting carried out. Bombardment of enemy's front & support lines during day - also wire cutting. Batteries very heavily shelled.	
	13/4/17	7·45 pm	Howitzers shelled HENDECOURT. Batteries continued wirecutting until ordered to stop. BULLECOURT bombarded by 81 Battery for 4 minutes at a time at 12 noon, 2·30 pm & 8·35 pm. Heavy Gun 1 pm - 3·30 pm. Batteries heavily shelled with 5·9s & 8 in. Heavy casualties to C/I Battery.	
	14/4/17		Shelled again at 4-4·30 pm & further casualties sustained. Military Medal awarded to O.S. Weatherly. A/312 Battery. Batteries carried out wirecutting around BULLECOURT & Howitzer Battery fired "raides" with Heavy Artillery. 18/pdr carried out bombardment at 7 pm. Practice barrage. Batteries heavily shelled during day.	
	15/4/17		Batteries fired in accordance with orders. Howitzer Battery fired crashes in co-operation with Heavy Artillery. Batteries again heavily shelled with guns of all calibres & gas shells.	
	16/4/17		Wire cutting carried out by A & B Batteries. Batteries again shelled.	Sd/

ORIGINAL

Army Form C. 2118.

WAR DIARY
of 312 Brigade R.F.A.
INTELLIGENCE SUMMARY. 1st Sheet
(Erase heading not required.)

Instructions regarding War Diaries and Intelligence Summaries are contained in F. S. Regs., Part II. and the Staff Manual respectively. Title pages will be prepared in manuscript.

Place	Date	Hour	Summary of Events and Information	Remarks and references to Appendices
VRAUCOURT	16/4/17		with 5.9's but no casualties reported.	
	17/4/17		Batteries carried on wirecutting + harasses fires appointed tasks. C/Battery went into rest for 24 hours as wagon lines. Night task firing on wire to prevent repairs.	
	18/4/17		B + D Batteries fired as per orders. Enemy shelled with gas shells B/Battery being relieved by C/Battery proceeded to wagon lines to rest.	
	19/4/17		A/Battery having 5 guns in action + C/Battery 3 - took over 3 from B/Battery and continued wirecutting. B/Battery proceeded to rest for 4 days. Taking all guns out to wagon lines to clean	
	20/4/17		Batteries continued firing on wire during day + night. B/Battery returned to action and A/Battery went out to rest.	
	21/4/17		Wire cutting continued. At 1.20 pm A + C Batteries fired in support of Army on our right.	
	22/4/17		Wire cutting continued and night firing on damaged wire.	
	23/4/17		Wire cutting continued. Batteries shelled heavily during day.	
	24/4/17		Day + Night firing as ordered on wire around BULLECOURT. A/Battery	HH

T2134. Wt. W708—776. 500000. 4/15. Sir J. C. & S.

ORIGINAL

Army Form C. 2118.

WAR DIARY of 312 Brigade RFA
INTELLIGENCE SUMMARY. 5th Sheet
(Erase heading not required.)

Instructions regarding War Diaries and Intelligence Summaries are contained in F. S. Regs., Part II. and the Staff Manual respectively. Title pages will be prepared in manuscript.

Place	Date	Hour	Summary of Events and Information	Remarks and references to Appendices
VRAUCOURT EAST	25/4/17		Returned from rest and C/Battery went out for further rest. A+B Batteries continued night firing as ordered.	
	26/4/17		A/Battery position shelled very heavily all night and up to 7.30pm with 5.9" and 4.2's causing damage to 2 guns and 8 casualties. Two NCO's and 27 other ranks reported wounded.	
	27/4/17		Battery position shell under heavy shell fire. 2 more guns put out of action. Traced in response to S.O.S. signal @ 5 am. B/Battery fired practice smoke barrage at 11 am – 11.8 am. 2334 Gnr A White awarded Military Medal.	
	28/4/17		Batteries subjected to heavy shelling during day causing casualties to A/Battery. B/Battery fired another smoke barrage + continued wire cutting. B/Battery being relieved by C/Battery went out to rest again.	
	29/4/17		A/Battery fired 100 rounds on defensive barrage in support of infantry. Battery shelled intermittently all day	
	30/4/17		Battery carried out day & night tasks as usual in Brigade zone. B/Battery guns came up into position. Brigade now had 16 guns for wire cutting dog trap [illegible]	

T2134. Wt. W708-776. 500000. 4/15. Sir J.C. & S.

SECRET

WAR DIARY
of
312 Brigade RFA

ORIGINAL

May 1st to May 31st.

WAR DIARY of 2nd Brigade RFA
INTELLIGENCE SUMMARY

Army Form C. 2118.

Place	Date	Hour	Summary of Events and Information	Remarks and references to Appendices
ECOUST	1/5/17		Batteries continued wire cutting. C/Battery brought up 3 guns but one hit during morning. Lieut A. D. GREEN from 35th Brigade RFA reported arrival	
	2/5/17	8am	Wire in Brigade gone. Reports under fire by day & night. Lt Col E. P. BEDWELL went up prison duty with 186th Infantry Brigade.	
	2/5/17	3.45 am	Brigade took part in attack on HINDENBURG LINE taking night front in rolling barrage as per orders issued in Brigade O.A. Instructions Sr 4 & 5 and firing was kept up all day	
		10.30 pm	Howitzers took part in bombardment of support trench & roads around BULLECOURT in support of 7th Durand Infantry attack on the village. 18 prs kept up steady fire from 10.30 pm to 11.45 pm on the BLUE line. A/Battery ceased fire at 11.30 pm	
			Lieut K. B. NICHOLSON granted Military Cross by H.M. The King. A/Bdr Queen & Driver Carlisle of B/Battery awarded Military Medal	
	4/4/17	4 am	Stores sent up near of 7th Division expected attack on Hindenburg Line & 15:00 Also fired in support lines for Ecoust. During the day Batteries fired as required by 7th Division.	

WAR DIARY
of 3/2 Brigade RFA
INTELLIGENCE SUMMARY.
(Erase heading not required.)

Sheet 2

Army Form C. 2118.

Place	Date	Hour	Summary of Events and Information	Remarks and references to Appendices
ECOUST	4/5/17	11.48 pm	B/B Battery fired on S.O.S. lines for 4 minutes. No enemy support line reply were fell during night.	
	5/5/17		Routine firing during day. At 9.50 pm Batteries fire schedule of fire in defence to S.O.S. for attack on AUSTRALIAN FRONT	
	4/5/17	4.10 am	Bombardment as follows by 18 pdrs Creeping fire on front line @ 40 rooms. Left 100 yards at 4.19 am at 13 am. Left 100 yards at 16 am. Left 100 yards beyond support trench. 4.19 am Left Back on front line at 5.2 am. Cease fire at 5.10 am. Rate of fire 3 rounds per gun from 8.15 am.	
		5.15	Double bombardment as follows Covered and by 15 pdrs. Open fire on front line 8.15 am. Left 100 yards 8.18 am - left to support line 8.21 am - Left Back on front line 8.24 am Cease fire 8.27 pm. Rate of fire 2 rounds per gun per minute. Otherwise no Dud Bombardment was added by 7 DA.	
	4/5/17	5.45 am	15 pdrs fired on trench U27.b.63 - O27.b.17 at 2 rds per gun per minute in support of attack of 7th Divison on BULLECOURT	
		4.45 am	Also enfilade on to trench U27 b.17 - U21 a.34 rate of fire 1 rd per gun per 30 mins + 5 am ok. am gun. During day Batteries kept up. Standing barrage in support of attacks of 7th Division.	

WAR DIARY of 312 Brigade RFA
INTELLIGENCE SUMMARY.
(Erase heading not required.)

Army Form C. 2118.

Place	Date	Hour	Summary of Events and Information	Remarks and references to Appendices
ECUST	7/5/17		A/Battery retired to new position at B.18.c.2 and B/Battery to B.18.c.37.	
	8/5/17		Batteries registered during morning. Howitzers fired as per notes of 7th MA	
			A/Battery again moved to position at B.15.c.27. & B/Battery to B.18.b.99	
	9/5/17		A & B Batteries registered in new positions. Aeroplane shot enemy carried out at 6 p.m. At 8 p.m. Batteries kept up slow rate of fire on S.O.S. lines.	
	10/5/17		Kept up fire on enemy support lines & approaches. At 7.30 p. fired for 15 minutes on S.O.S. lines.	
	11/5/17		Kept up day & night tasks as per notes. Howitzer fired as per notes from 7th DA. Standing Barrage commenced at 3.40 am 12/5/17 in support	
	12/5/17		of Infantry. Day & night firing as ordered. HQs shelled heavily during afternoon 2 casualties.	
	13/5/17	3.40 am	Fired from 3.40 am to 3.50 am @ 2 rds per gun per minute in support of 7th Div. Infantry. During day C & D batteries registered on new zone. S.O.S. at night and batteries were heavily shelled	
	14/5/17		Day & night tasks.	
	15/5/17		with gas shells & 5.9s. Slow rate of fire maintained on S.O.S. lines during night. Day and during afternoon HQs was reduced to kinds of fire	

Army Form C. 2118.

WAR DIARY
of 312 Brigade R.F.A.
INTELLIGENCE SUMMARY
(Erase heading not required.)

Place	Date	Hour	Summary of Events and Information	Remarks and references to Appendices
ECOUST-ST-MEIN	15/3/17		Lt Col E.P. BEDWELL admitted to 47 C.C.S - sick. Major G.R. FLEMING took over temporary command of Brigade.	
	16/3/17		No firing done during morning but Minenwerfers and one 15cm (C152) fired during afternoon.	
	17/3/17		Major F.H. ISTER D.S.O. R.A. took over command of Brigade. Day and night routine firing.	
	18/3/17		One of 3) old culverts sent HATCHER & LINTERN arrived. Routine firing during day and night.	
	19/3/17		Routine firing on back areas by day & night.	
	20/3/17		Fired on targets in back areas by day and night.	
	21/3/17 3.20 a.m		No. 3 Bde A.O.K. fired in operations on BOIS TRENCH which were unsuccessful.	
			Routine firing during day on targets in back areas. Inch roads & enemy parties.	
	22/3/17		Routine firing on targets in back areas.	
			Long report	
	23/3/17		Day & night firing on roads and tracks in back area.	
	24/3/17		Routine firing on roads, tracks and targets in back area.	
	25/3/17		Routine firing on targets in back area.	

Army Form C. 2118.

WAR DIARY
of 312 Brigade RFA
INTELLIGENCE SUMMARY.
(Erase heading not required.)

Sheet 5

Place	Date	Hour	Summary of Events and Information	Remarks and references to Appendices
ECOUST ST-MEIN	26/5/17	1.30pm	Fired on roads & tracks in enemy area. Explosion of ammunition dump at D/Battery causing death of 2/Capt H.B. GALLIMORE and 10 Other Ranks. Lieut G. HARDY and 3 other ranks severely wounded. The explosion was caused by a spark from a gun which was near the "raffia" fishing net camouflage covering the gun pit camp and the charge hung up. Meantime Officers and Nos. 1 turned up to extinguish it with earth and spades and 3 minutes after the fire began the shells blew up. One gun shield and carriage destroyed another gun slightly damaged. In consequence of this accident O.R.A. Gen Division has ordered that in future when fire occurs on 4.5" battery the area should be got clear or under cover and not attempt to extinguish this nature of ammunition.	
	27/5/17		Usual routine firing on roads and tracks on trek area. Organised shell holes in enemys line fired on. Enemy bombers in Lines at U.22.c.55 and U.22.b.21. Shooting restricted by Group Orders. 2/Lt G. HARDY died of his wounds at an C.C.S. F.M.	
	28/5/17		Routine firing day and night. Enemy movement in SUNKEN ROAD about U.23.b.48 dealt with by D/Battery. Shell holes occupied about U.23.d.07	

T2134. Wt. W708—776. 500000. 4/15. Sir J. C. & S.

Army Form C. 2118.

WAR DIARY
of 312 Brigade RFA
INTELLIGENCE SUMMARY.
Sheet 6
(Erase heading not required.)

Place	Date	Hour	Summary of Events and Information	Remarks and references to Appendices
ECOUST-ST-MEIN	29/8/17		Shelled by 18 pr Batteries. Enemy aircraft very active during week in early hours of morning undeterred by our aircraft.	
	29/8/17		Ranche Battery on hostile battery at U18c 51 and cross roads at U17a 35 and on SUNKEN ROAD U17d 46 to U17d 10.2½ also Pioneer Dump U24a69. Enemy party of known coming from REINCOURT to trench U24 central engaged & dispersed, again at 9.45 am and 3.10 pm parties were seen moving at U24 d 38. Engaged & dispersed by A/312 Battery.	
	30/8/17		Ranche Battery on trench - railway in U22 k. Shell hole V22 c 45 to V22 b 21 Pioneer Dump at U24a69 and O.P in V23 k.	
	31/8/17		Ranche Battery on targets in back areas	

J.H. Winter Major RFA
Comdg 312 Bde
BFA

Original

Vol 6

War Diary

of

312th Brigade, R.F.A.

Volume VI

From 1st June 1917
To 30th June 1917.

ORIGINAL

WAR DIARY
INTELLIGENCE SUMMARY. 3/2 Brigade RFA
Sheet I

Army Form C. 2118.

Place	Date	Hour	Summary of Events and Information	Remarks and references to Appendices
ECOUST ST-DEIN	1/6/17		Routine Our M targets in back areas.	
	2/6/17		Routine fire on back areas, approaches and roads from 10.30 – 11.30. 18 pdr Batteries fired T.S. Barrage on Hindenburg support line in U22c & d.	
	3/6/17		Usual fire on tgts in back area. At 8pm 2/3 Bn 173 Infantry Brigade reported much movement in HENDECOURT CHATEAU WOOD. Within 4 minutes of receipt of this 16 pdr salvos were fired in it with good effects.	
	4/6/17		Routine fire on back areas during night. D/312 fired on machine gun emplacement from 8.30 – 9.30 am and carried out registration in U20b from 9.30 am to 11 am. Enemy to batteries being under direct observation of enemy balloons no firing was done during fore- & afternoon. New tgts observed and registration in U15c 16.20 and U.15c 85.60 and also U.15 d.15.45. By aeroplane observation. Routine fire by 18pdrs.	
	5/6/17	23/P	S.A.S. reed V.14 d.15 .45	
	6/6/17		Routine fire on back areas	
	7/6/17		Day & night tasks as follows. Machine guns in O23 d 75.10 – 45.40 – O22 b 20.0 Cross roads at U17 a 35 35, U18 d O1 & machine gun at U23 b 74 and Howitzer in tracks in U17 a. Howitzers also fired at enemy seen in the open at U15 but range was too great	

ORIGINAL

Army Form C. 2118.

WAR DIARY
of 32 Brigade RFA Sheet II
INTELLIGENCE SUMMARY.
(Erase heading not required.)

Instructions regarding War Diaries and Intelligence Summaries are contained in F.S. Regs, Part II. and the Staff Manual respectively. Title pages will be prepared in manuscript.

Place	Date	Hour	Summary of Events and Information	Remarks and references to Appendices
ECOUST ST-MEIN	8/6/17		Firing during day & night on machine gun emplacements at U.16.b.02.20, U.16.b.b. U.22.b.20.4, V.27.B. 75.10.45.48, V.17.b.25.50 and on SUNKEN ROAD and forming shell holes in U.23 and U.24. Wiring parties at U.22.b.74 & U.22.c.46 thoroughly fired on. Tracks at U.17.d.	
	9/6/17	11.30 pm 11.30 pm	Barrage fire in support of raid on the KNUCKLE.	
	9/6/17		Routine firing on back areas, machine gun emplacements & shell hole. During these two days hostile shelling has been practically nil, and movement has been confined to single parties.	
	10/6/17		Routine fire on targets in back areas. Owing to bad visibility observation was poor and effect of fire was not observed. 1 Cpl E P BEDWELL executed to England and struck off strength of Brigade from 1st June 1917.	
	11/6/17		Firing on back areas by 18 pdrs. 2/3.12 night firing on CRUMP ALLEY and enemy retaliated on our front line when Stokes opened fire.	
	12/6/17		Firing on targets in back areas by day & night.	

T2134. Wt. W708—776. 500000. 4/15. Sir J. C. & S.

ORIGINAL

Army Form C. 2118.

Instructions regarding War Diaries and Intelligence Summaries are contained in F. S. Regs., Part II. and the Staff Manual respectively. Title pages will be prepared in manuscript.

WAR DIARY
of 312 Brigade RFA
INTELLIGENCE SUMMARY. Sheet III
(Erase heading not required.)

Place	Date	Hour	Summary of Events and Information	Remarks and references to Appendices
ECOUST ST-MEIN	13/6/17	3.5 – 3.5am	Sniped bombardment in HINDENBURG LINE in Co-operation with Corps Heavy Artillery. During the day targets and hosts in back kept under continuous fire.	
	14/6/17	2.15 am	Barrage fired by B/312 in conjunction with raid on BOVIS TRENCH. All Batteries registered G.F. on Zero line and points on extreme right + left however. Returns fire on targets in back areas	
	15/6/17	3.0 am – 12.30 pm	by 173 H/ Bde. Barrages an Attack [crossed out] an attack on HINDENBURG first Line. Sh Lharry registered with those being barrages from U.14.c.2.5 to U.20.c.4.2 (NW of BULLECOURT). All batteries engaged in the barrage, (with "creeping and back" 'flash' barrage. (Operations carried out under 58th Div Arty Op. Order No 10) Attack completely successful 43 prisoners taken.	
		9 pm	German counter attacked and retook part of his front line. S.O.S. was fired 3 times between this and 11 pm. Situation was then hathin of ease.	
	16.6.17	2.10	According to Op. Order No 11 of 58 Inf Bde attack was delivered to capture the HINDENBURG Support line, by 173 Inf Bde from U.14.a.7.1 to U.20.c.5.7. A special barrage to precede & accompany of front line was ordered, but later cancelled as unnecessary & attack as ordered was carried out. 312 Bde 18 Pr Batteries in flank barrage, xD/312 in How creeping	

ORIGINAL

Army Form C. 2118.

WAR DIARY
of 312 Brigade R.F.A.
INTELLIGENCE SUMMARY. Sheet IV
(Erase heading not required.)

Instructions regarding War Diaries and Intelligence Summaries are contained in F.S. Regs., Part II. and the Staff Manual respectively. Title pages will be prepared in manuscript.

Place	Date	Hour	Summary of Events and Information	Remarks and references to Appendices
	16.6.17 cont		Barrage. Attack only partially successful, portions of support line being gained and held. Intermittent fire kept up all day as German reinforcements were seen at intervals coming over the ridge in U.14 and 15. – No systematic counter-battery work undertaken by enemy either earlier or yet, the E COAST rally was promiscuously strafed for an hour in the morning. Weather v. hot – a clear, thick heat haze. On SOS. was received from front of attack about 7 pm. 312 Bde continued their special task of strafing an area (practically square Q.15) all night – kept the wise quiet. Further fire during day by C+D Batteries.	JKL
	17.6.17	9.15 am	Bourke Battery engaged by D/312 at V.a.4. (Aeroplane Target) D/312 had an ammunition pit let dry hostile fire and an iron pit out of action. This battery was very accurately shelled, as well as an 18 pr. but on it left, with 105mm with very instantaneous fuze, from 7am to 4pm. – This is the first counter-battery work done by the enemy in connection with the fighting of 15 to 16th. – It seems as tho' he has not guns enough here to deal with our infantry & artillery adequately at the same time. All quiet.	
	18th 19th		At noon orders were recd for the 312 Bde to start relieving 91st Bde (20th D.A.)	JML

ORIGINAL

Army Form C. 2118.

WAR DIARY of 312 Brigade RFA

INTELLIGENCE SUMMARY. Sheet V

(Erase heading not required.)

Place	Date	Hour	Summary of Events and Information	Remarks and references to Appendices
	19/6/17	10pm to 12pm	In the QUÉANT front on night 19/7/20 to relief to be completed by 8 am 22nd. One section from each Battery 312 Bde moved off and relieved sections of 91st Bde 7/12 relieving A91-B312, D91,- C312 C91, B312 D91.	FK
	20	10 to 12pm	"D" Battery position in Scout Valley again shelled by 4.2" at intervals during the day. A few this section /A & C batteries retired sections of 91st Bde D battery took over & all their ammunition & was completed the relief of D91.	
	21		D Battery evacuated by on shelled intermittently during the day. D91 dead the remaining guns of A91 C batteries were since out and the relief of 91st Bde batteries completed. Battery positions A312 C23a 55.60 with a forward Gun at C93 K.2.3, B312 C28d.2.5, C312 C27b.65.5, D312 C29c.0.9 312 Bde forth over from 91st Head quarters 312 Bde moved to C26d.1.6. OC 312 Bde in command of Right Group. 20 Div Arty consisting of A B & D batteries 312 Bde and 4th Australian Bde	
	22	8AM		

WAR DIARY
or INTELLIGENCE SUMMARY
of 312 Brigade R.F.A. Sheet VI

Place	Date	Hour	Summary of Events and Information	Remarks and references to Appendices
	20/6/17		Consisting of 53rd Bty (out at rest) 54# 55# 114# (How.) Btys. C.312 Bde. Came under the command of 310 Bde forming the left group. From observation of enemy country it appears that he has not been much harassed by artillery fire during the hours of daylight. Considerable movement of large parties at ranges of 4000 to 5000 yards from battery positions.	
	23		Began lines moved to H.14 and H.24 b. Nineteen lately occupied by 91 Bde. Considerable movement observed from Battery O.P.s but owing to enemy observation Lilloors, batteries were not able to open fire. At noon the command of the artillery covering the 20th Divisional front passed to the 62nd Div. Bty. Vicinity of Steenwerck from J.A.3.12 heavily shelled by 4"6.2" Steenwerck all quiet.	
	24			
	25		All quiet. 60 inf. Bde covered by right group artillery	

ORIGINAL

Army Form C. 2118.

WAR DIARY
or 312 Brigade R.F.A.
INTELLIGENCE SUMMARY. April 1917

(Erase heading not required.)

Instructions regarding War Diaries and Intelligence Summaries are contained in F.S. Regs., Part II. and the Staff Manual respectively. Title pages will be prepared in manuscript.

Place	Date	Hour	Summary of Events and Information	Remarks and references to Appendices
	23/4/17 26		relieved by 185 inf Bde. A fine day. Observation very poor. D battery Brestow evidently shifted, shelled intermittently for 18 hours by 10.30 am hr. Two guns knocked out. Enemy artillery very quiet on the rest of our front. Australian artillery Bde. intends to withdraw from action. When this Brigade is withdrawn C/312 battery will form right group 62 Div Arty Right Group (312 Bde RFA) covering regrouped infantry brigade in the line from D20 b 0.8 to C 12 b 0.7.	
	27	10pm	See section of each battery 14th Bde withdrawn. All quiet. The remaining guns 14th Bde were withdrawn C/312 battery now in Left Group joining right group 62 D.A. 186 infantry brigade relieved left infantry brigade 20th Div in the line.	
	28		Hot close day. Violent Thunderstorm in the evening. Hostile artillery again very quiet.	

ORIGINAL

Army Form C. 2118.

WAR DIARY
or of 812 Brigade 274
INTELLIGENCE SUMMARY. Sheet VIII
(Erase heading not required.)

Place	Date	Hour	Summary of Events and Information	Remarks and references to Appendices
	29/6/15	30	All quiet— Another quiet day. B and C batteries moved a single gun to previous positions. The bulk of the shooting will be done by these two guns and the forward guns of A battery. The remaining guns of the batteries will to a great extent be kept for defensive purposes.	

HLutu Sewer

Original

SECRET No 7

Confidential
War Diary
of
312th Brigade R.F.A.

from 1st July 1917 — to 31st July 1917

No. Vol. VII

ORIGINAL

WAR DIARY
of 312 Brigade R.F.A.
INTELLIGENCE SUMMARY
Sheet 1

Army Form C. 2118.

Place	Date	Hour	Summary of Events and Information	Remarks and references to Appendices
	July 1st		A more active policy is being adopted, any enemy seen within range of the three forward guns and by the batteries if the situation permits (no enemy batteries up) are immediately fired on. During the day batteries engaged the enemy whenever a target was offered. Several hundred rounds were fired. The forward guns of A and C batteries were not shelled but B battery gun received considerable attention from a 4.2 battery and was withdrawn at night. The howitzer policy was intermittent firing with considerable success and the slight retaliation that followed was mostly directed against LAGNICOURT. Orders received to move B3/2 battery to a position in 13d. The position they are occupying will be taken over by D293 Bde who will come under the command of the Lt.Col. Group. 62 D.A. A two gun battery D293 Bde will relief a position either L.6, 9.8 or L28, b.60 and be under the command of the right group, they will come	DA

ORIGINAL

WAR DIARY
or ¬~~Intelligence~~/SUMMARY
of 7/312 Brigade R.FA

Army Form C. 2118.

Sheet — 11

Instructions regarding War Diaries and Intelligence Summaries are contained in F.S. Regs., Part II. and the Staff Manual respectively. Title pages will be prepared in manuscript.

Place	Date	Hour	Summary of Events and Information	Remarks and references to Appendices
	2/7/17		into action on the night 3/4th July. C/293 will relieve one section C/312 on the night 3/4th July and the remainder 4/5th July. All quiet. D/312 only having 3 guns in action. D/293 battery will not bring their section into action but hand over their three guns to D/312. This will take place on the night 4/5th July. D/393 battery personnel remaining at their wagon lines. Orders received that all batteries 293 Brigade will come under the command of 62 Division. The relief of C/312 Bde by C/293 Bde will take place on the nights 4/5th July and 5/6th July and not as previously ordered. D/293 every such action complete on the night 5/6th July will form the 'Howitzer Group' battery position 25-d.5.1. Another section may me section C/312 Bde relieved by a section of C/293 Bde. The former coming into action at 25-d.4.3	
	4			

ORIGINAL

Army Form C. 2118.

WAR DIARY
or 312 Brigade R.F.A.
INTELLIGENCE SUMMARY. Sheet III

(Erase heading not required.)

Instructions regarding War Diaries and Intelligence Summaries are contained in F. S. Regs., Part II. and the Staff Manual respectively. Title pages will be prepared in manuscript.

Place	Date	Hour	Summary of Events and Information	Remarks and references to Appendices
	5-7-17		Very accurate shelling of D/312 battery position by a 4.2" battery. Two guns put out of action and gun pits badly damaged. The relief of C/312 battery completed & we decided to move D/312 battery position selected at C.29.a.0.8. for four guns, and work commence there.	
	6		Headquarters 312 Brigade moved forward to new quarters C.29.a.5.1 in order to be in closer liaison with the Infantry Brigade H.Q. situated at C.29.a.4.1	
	7		All quiet. wet day and observation bad & our batteries unable to carry out their usual programme of harassing all movement of the enemy in their lines	
	8		Lt. Col. A.F. Pugh takes over command of 312 Brigade and Major Jump from Lt. Col. F.H. Foster D.S.O. posted to G.H.Q.	
	9		D/312 battery return the forward howitzer to D/293 battery the latter coming into action with this section at C.29.a.2.7	MP
	10			

ORIGINAL

Army Form C. 2118.

WAR DIARY or Intelligence M.7A
INTELLIGENCE SUMMARY. Sheet No. IV
(Erase heading not required.)

Place	Date	Hour	Summary of Events and Information	Remarks and references to Appendices
	10.7.17		A quiet day	
	11		Another quiet day. The M./M. Group consisting of 4.18 pounder Batteries A 312, B 312, C 312, A 298 and Two 4.5 howitzer Batteries D 312 D 298 (2 guns) expend ammunition as follows 18 pounders 1000 rounds 4.5 How. 300 rounds per diem. 70% this allotment is fired at night. Batteries are all to do more day shooting now as enemy balloon observation is considerably reduced.	
	12		Enemy aircraft very active during the day and met with little opposition. Orders received that A 293 Bde are to leave this Group. They moved out at dusk necessitating a re-adjustment of our defensive lines A 312 Battery very accurately shelled by a 4".2 Battery about 100 rounds between 9.30 am and 10.30 am. No damage	
	13		6 guns out-dug-outs damaged and 2 men wounded	1742

ORIGINAL

WAR DIARY or **INTELLIGENCE SUMMARY.**

Army Form C. 2118.

of J 312 Brigade R.F.A. Sheet V

Place	Date	Hour	Summary of Events and Information	Remarks and references to Appendices
	14.7.17		A quiet day very close and hot, heavy thunder rain at night.	
	15		A rather fine quiet day. Included in the night shoot a small gas bombardment of sheds and dugouts in D9c5.9 filled up later by heavy bursts by fire from 4.5" hows and 18 pounders	
	16		A very uneventful day except for a rather heavy shelling of batteries by a 4.2" battery. Enemy artillery were very quiet on our front. Our infantry raided an enemy post calling on the artillery to support their return at 3.45 am a barrage was put up at a slow rate lasting 30 minutes. At 4.15 am received a SOS call from the 8th Infantry Brigade on our right. Support was given with #18 bohm. and 2 howitzers until 4.30 am when all became quiet	
	17		A quiet day. Mem received to reduce the expenditure of ammunition to 130 rounds per 18pdr battery and	M

ORIGINAL

Army Form C. 2118.

Instructions regarding War Diaries and Intelligence
Summaries are contained in F. S. Regs., Part II.
and the Staff Manual respectively. Title pages
will be prepared in manuscript.

WAR DIARY
of 312 Brigade R.F.A
INTELLIGENCE SUMMARY. Sheet No VI
(Erase heading not required.)

Place	Date	Hour	Summary of Events and Information	Remarks and references to Appendices
	17/7/17		75 rounds per 4.5" howitzer battery	
	18		All quiet. Heavy rain at night. Batteries inspected by G.O.C. 3rd Army. Complimented by him on the cleanliness and activity of the batteries.	
	19		All quiet. Bombarded Lens with 4.5" chemical shell at 1.30 am. A normal day. Batteries did little shooting in order to keep within the limits of ammunition allotted for the week.	
	20		A 312 battery at C.93.a.3.3 heavily shelled from dawn to 11am. About 400 rounds 4.2" fell near the battery. Two guns (Nos 2 and 3) put out of action and considerable ammunition destroyed. No casualties to personnel. At 10pm Sainhem road at Bois de Hirondelle was heavily shelled for 8 minutes. A 4.2 battery and intermittent fire was continued on it. hourly until 6am the morning from 9pm till 11pm C 312 battery C/93.d.4.3 received considerable attention from a 4.2" battery. 3 gun pits were hit no guns were put out	JWL

T2134. Wt. W708–770. 500000. 4/15. Sir J. C. & S.

ORIGINAL

Army Form C. 2118.

WAR DIARY
of 312 Brigade RFA
INTELLIGENCE SUMMARY.
(Erase heading not required.) Sheet No. VII

Instructions regarding War Diaries and Intelligence Summaries are contained in F. S. Regs., Part II. and the Staff Manual respectively. Title pages will be prepared in manuscript.

Place	Date	Hour	Summary of Events and Information	Remarks and references to Appendices
	22.7.17		No action and there were no casualties to personnel. All quiet. It was decided to move C 312 Battery from its present position. One section moved to a new position at J.11.b.75.85.	
	23		The remaining section of C Battery was moved to the new position. The forward gun was also moved to a prepared position at C.24.c.05.20	
	24		All quiet. Sent out a new one in order preparation of C.92.d.5.5 antialle and a new one in order preparation of C.92.d.5.5. B.312 Battery's forward gun moved to a prepared position at C.23.d.4.9	
	25		Dull morning, fine later. A very quiet day.	
	26		Rather more hostile shelling than usual. From 6 to 12 enemy balloons up all day. Enemy aeroplanes very active from 4 pm to dusk. Infantry raids on enemy front, out and enemy several strong patrols which they engaged but failed to take.	101

T2134. Wt. W708—776. 500000. 4/15. Sir J. C. & S.

ORIGINAL

Army Form C. 2118.

WAR DIARY of 312 Brigade RFA
INTELLIGENCE SUMMARY Sheet No. VIII
(Erase heading not required.)

Instructions regarding War Diaries and Intelligence Summaries are contained in F. S. Regs., Part II. and the Staff Manual respectively. Title pages will be prepared in manuscript.

Place	Date	Hour	Summary of Events and Information	Remarks and references to Appendices
	27/7/17		any prisoners, a slight 18 pounder barrage was put down to cover their retreat.	
	28		C Battery's forward gun at C24 c 05.20 heavily shelled from 2 pm to 6 pm by 5.9" gun and 4.2" mortar about 200 rounds in all. No casualties to gun or personnel.	
	29		Very heavy rain and thunderstorm during the morning and early afternoon. Hostile barrage commenced at C24 C 2.1 on gun pits to the two howitzers at D 20.3. The 186 Infantry Brigade covered by the howitzer group of Divisional Artillery will be relieved tonight by the 184 Infantry Brigade.	
	30		A dull day all quiet.	
	31		Another dull day, with heavy rain at night. After nine days interval "A" 312 Battery position was again heavily shelled by 150 m.m mortar battery about 200 rounds fell near the Battery position. One direct hit and the gun put out of action. No casualties to personnel.	ML

L. Albrigh? Lieut RFA
Commanding 312 Bde RFA

SECRET

Vol 8

War Diary

312 Brigade R.F.A.

Original

Volume VIII

From 1st August 1917
To 31st August 1917

ORIGINAL

WAR DIARY
or
INTELLIGENCE SUMMARY.

Army Form C. 2118.

of 312 Brigade R.F.A

Sheet I

(Erase heading not required.)

Instructions regarding War Diaries and Intelligence Summaries are contained in F.S. Regs., Part II. and the Staff Manual respectively. Title pages will be prepared in manuscript.

Place	Date	Hour	Summary of Events and Information	Remarks and references to Appendices
SAILLY-AU-BOIS	1/8/17 2		All quiet, heavy shower during the day. During the afternoon crashes were fired into Bramelle by hy bty Group artillery and answered by "Left Group" artillery. Retaliation followed.	
	3		All quiet, wet day. Orders received for the Hy Group artillery reodjustments. C/312 Bde will relieve B/293 Bde. B/312 Bde will interchange with A/293 Bde. C/312 Bde will interchange with C/293 Bde. One section to be moved each night, 4/5th Aug, 5/6th and 6/7th August. D/312 will move into complete on the ng ht 6/7th August to their wagon lines and commence work on a new position at B/12.	
	4		Another wet day. Ground very heavy. It was decided on the case of A/312 that as interchange of positions will take place with B/293. That they should occupy their new positions under construction at C.22 d 5.5. C/312 Bde and C/293 Bde have mutually agreed not to move their guns but to exchange pieces	JAL

T2134. Wt. W708-776. 50000. 4/15. Sir J. C. & S.

ORIGINAL

Army Form C. 2118.

WAR DIARY of 312 Brigade R.F.A
INTELLIGENCE SUMMARY. Sheet No 4

(Erase heading not required.)

Instructions regarding War Diaries and Intelligence Summaries are contained in F. S. Regs., Part II. and the Staff Manual respectively. Title pages will be prepared in manuscript.

Place	Date	Hour	Summary of Events and Information	Remarks and references to Appendices
	4.8.17		B/312 Bde will carry out the interchange as ordered. The move of one section B/312 and C/312 (personnel) completed. A further section of B and C/312 moved over, one section D/312 moved to wagon lines.	
	5			
	6		The interchange of Brigades completed and new guns of fire taken over. The remaining Howitzers of D/312 moved to their wagon lines.	
	7		Headquarters 312 Brigade moved to their wagon lines Bulgerstown. 29 ○ Brigade moving in and taking over the command of the Laprécaut Sector under the 8rd Division. The relief was completed at 9 a.m. The 62nd Divisional Front will now be as follows NOREIL Sector covered by "Right Group" 62nd D.A. composed as follows 4 batteries 310 Bde and two batteries (A and C) 312 Bde under Lt. Col. Sherlock. BULLECOURT Sector covered by "Left Group" 62nd DA composed as follows 4 batteries 35th Bde and two batteries (B and D) 312 Bde	JNL

T2134. Wt. W708—776. 500000. 4/15. Sir J. C. & S.

WAR DIARY of 312 Brigade RFA
INTELLIGENCE SUMMARY

Sheet No. III

Army Form C. 2118.

ORIGINAL

Instructions regarding War Diaries and Intelligence Summaries are contained in F. S. Regs., Part II. and the Staff Manual respectively. Title pages will be prepared in manuscript.

Place	Date	Hour	Summary of Events and Information	Remarks and references to Appendices
	7.8.17		ande Lt-Col Macfarlane	
	8		The Battery positions 312 Brigade RFA are now as follows A312 C92d5.5 B312 C9a2.6 C312 C9d6.6 D312 will not go into action until their howitzers have been overhauled at the repair shops. In the meantime they will prepare a forward position for a section of C9C1.3	
	9		Works on the construction of winter standings has been commenced at the wagon lines. Orders received that these are to be completed by the end of September. Additional labour put on this work.	
	10		From 10th to 22nd this Brigade headquarters remained out of action of their wagon lines	
	22		Orders received that the 95th Brigade will move out of the line on the nights 23/24 and 24/25 August and will be relieved by batteries of 312 Brigade. On completion of the relief this "L.of.C.Group" 62nd RFA will come under the command of Lt-Col St Pugh	ALL

ORIGINAL

Army Form C. 2118.

WAR DIARY
or
312 Brigade R7A
INTELLIGENCE SUMMARY. Sheet No IV
(Erase heading not required.)

Place	Date	Hour	Summary of Events and Information	Remarks and references to Appendices
	23.8.17		Preparations made for the move of 312 Brigade Headquarters	
	24		Brigade headquarters moved to L'Homme Mort B.14.b.2.6	
			The relief of 35 Brigade was completed at midnight	
	25		312 Brigade from the "Soft group" 62nd DA covering the Bullecourt sector. The Battery Positions are A.312 Bam position C.7.c.75.25 forward gun at C.8.a.5.8 B.312 Bam position C.7.a.28 forward gun at C.2.a.5.3 D.312 Bam position C.13.a.3.7 forward section C.2.c.1.3	
	26		All quiet, batteries registered Datum points, S.O.S. lines and various targets	
	27		All quiet save in the morning turning to cold and rain later	
	28		All quiet - heavy rain	
	29		Slight hostile shelling of Ecourt and Bullecourt	
	30		All quiet - heavy showers	
	31		All quiet	JHL

J- Obright Lr Col R.F.A.
Commanding 312 Bde R.F.A.

Original

War Diary
of
312th Brigade, R.F.A.

Volume IX

From 1st September 1917
To 30th September 1917

Army Form C. 2118.

WAR DIARY
or ~~INTELLIGENCE SUMMARY.~~

of J/312 Brigade R.F.A   ORIGINAL   Sheet No. 1

(Erase heading not required.)

Instructions regarding War Diaries and Intelligence Summaries are contained in F. S. Regs., Part II. and the Staff Manual respectively. Title pages will be prepared in manuscript.

Place	Date	Hour	Summary of Events and Information	Remarks and references to Appendices
	September 1st 1917		All Quiet	
	2		Slight hostile shelling of 5 COUST and BULLECOURT	
	3		All Quiet. Concentration on BULLDOG support trench 400 by 6" Hows 300 rounds by D/312 Battery	
	4		All Quiet	
	5		All Quiet. Concentration ordered for tonight and following night on enemy front line trench in K.23.c and to be carried out	
	6		All Quiet. Orders received to save ammunition out of the existing allotment of ammunition viz 330 rounds 18 pdr and 150 rounds 4.5" Hows per day. About 150 rounds 18 pdr will be under ht	
	7		All Quiet. Orders received to reduce the ammunition as the gun fire from 300 to 200 rounds per 18 pdr and from 200 to 100 rounds per 4.5" Howitzer. A/312 Move a section forwards to B.22.c.2.5	
	8		Hostile Shelling above normal	
	9		All Quiet. 2/Lt. T. Hay leaves B/312 Battery for Base Depot	
	10		Hostile fire above normal. D/312 Move a section forward to C.22.C.1.3. JWL	

T2134. Wt. W708—776. 500000. 4/15. Sir J. C. & S.

WAR DIARY or INTELLIGENCE SUMMARY

Army Form C. 2118.

Sir F 912 Brigade RFA
Sheet No 11
ORIGINAL

Place	Date	Hour	Summary of Events and Information	Remarks and references to Appendices
	10/7/17		All quiet. 62nd Divisional Artillery put up a barrage in support of a raid on enemy trenches on U.23.d. Two prisoners taken and barrage reported very effective	
	12		All quiet during the day	
	13		At 4 am the enemy put down a heavy barrage on our infantry posts in U.23 and U.29. At 5 am he raided and entered our posts. Light group artillery answered a S.O.S call at 4.5 am and continued to keep up a slow rate of fire until 5.10 am	
	14		All quiet. Concentrated at 10 pm on headquarters at U.24.b.3.4. 100 rounds 4.5" How. lethal and 100 rounds 18 pdr H.E.	
	15		All quiet, bright fine day	
	16		All quiet	
	17		11.30 am to noon enemy fire put down in trench mortars which were employed in a destructive shoot on enemy front line trenches. Concentrated on Reincourt at 9.30, 10.15 & 11 pm	JW

Army Form C. 2118.

WAR DIARY
or
INTELLIGENCE SUMMARY.

of 312 Brigade RFA Sheet No III
ORIGINAL
(Erase heading not required.)

Instructions regarding War Diaries and Intelligence Summaries are contained in F. S. Regs., Part II. and the Staff Manual respectively. Title pages will be prepared in manuscript.

Place	Date	Hour	Summary of Events and Information	Remarks and references to Appendices
	18/9/17		All quiet during the day. fine.	
	19/9/17		All quiet. fine. The 62nd Divisional Artillery in conjunction with the Trench Mortars and Corps Heavy Artillery carried out a bombardment of the enemy front line trenches	
	20/9/17		At 4 a.m. the enemy bombarded our front line trenches. In response to an S.O.S. call the 62nd Divisional Artillery fired on their S.O.S. lines. A slow rate of fire being maintained until 5-10 a.m. when all was reported quiet. From 3.29 pm to 4 pm the 62nd Divil. Artillery 18 pounder batteries put down covering fire for the Trench Mortars who carried out a destructive shoot on the enemy front line.	
	21/9/17		All quiet a fine day.	
	22/9/17		All quiet fine, during the day. At 10 to 10.17 p.m. the enemy bombarded our front line At 10.15 pm 62nd Divisional Artillery assisted by Corps Heavy Artillery put down a crash on RIENCOURT with good effect.	
	23/9/17		All quiet. A fine clear day.	
	24/9/17		All quiet. fine. The 62nd Divisional Artillery in conjunction with Trench Mortars and Corps Heavy Artillery carried out a bombardment of enemy front and support line trenches and suspected Trench Mortar emplacements.	SCF

Army Form C. 2118.

WAR DIARY
or
INTELLIGENCE SUMMARY.

of 312 Brigade RFA
Sheet No IV

ORIGINAL

(Erase heading not required.)

Place	Date	Hour	Summary of Events and Information	Remarks and references to Appendices
	25/9/17		All quiet during the day. Fine.	
	26/9/17		Special Bombardment of enemy front and support lines by 312 Bde in conjunction with 310Bde. Corps Heavy Artillery and Trench mortars during the night the whole the 4 & 5 hows 312 Brigade assisted in a bombardment using lethal shell.	
	27/9/17		A fine day. A/312 Battery position heavily shelled at intervals throughout the day.	
	28/9/17		All quiet. Fine. 2nd Lt C.B. Snoise leaves A/312 on transfer to Divisional Trench Mortars	
	29/9/17		All quiet. Fine.	
	30/9/17		All quiet. Fine.	

J. J. Stephenson Lt Col
Cmdg 312 Bde RFA

Secret   Original

Vol 10

War Diary

of

312th Brigade R.F.A

Volume X

From 1st October 1917
To 31st October 1917

ORIGINAL

WAR DIARY
of 312 Brigade Royal Field Artillery
INTELLIGENCE SUMMARY.
(Erase heading not required.) Sheet I

Army Form C. 2118.

Instructions regarding War Diaries and Intelligence Summaries are contained in F. S. Regs., Part II. and the Staff Manual respectively. Title pages will be prepared in manuscript.

Place	Date	Hour	Summary of Events and Information	Remarks and references to Appendices
October	1/10/14		All quiet, dull day.	
	2/10/14		Another quiet day.	
	3/10/14		Two enemy trench howitzers on Frond Line trenches, silenced by B/312 Bde. Tour Trench and Bullecourt heavily shelled for 30 minutes by enemy 77 m.m. and 105 m.m. batteries.	
	4/10/14		Hostile artillery very quiet, wet night.	
	5/10/14 7pm		Lethal shell bombardment of enemy dugouts by D battery. Enemy trench mortars engaged and silenced by D battery.	
	6/10/14		All quiet, wet day.	
	7/10/14		D/312 engaged two enemy trench mortars with good effect. Vacated battery position in C8a heavily shelled by enemy 105 m.m. battery, about 300 rounds, shooting rather erratic.	
	8/10/14		All quiet & very wet night.	
	9/10/14		Wire cut & several bombs on enemy wire covering Boris Trench. 9.45pm a covering fire put down in support of an enemy carrying raid on this Trench. Enemy replied with a short but heavy	

ORIGINAL

Army Form C. 2118.

WAR DIARY
of J 312 Brigade RFA
INTELLIGENCE/SUMMARY. Aug & II
(Erase heading not required.)

Instructions regarding War Diaries and Intelligence Summaries are contained in F.S. Regs., Part II. and the Staff Manual respectively. Title pages will be prepared in manuscript.

Place	Date	Hour	Summary of Events and Information	Remarks and references to Appendices
October	9th 1917		Barrage on our front line trenches at 10 p.m.	
	10.10.17		Hostile artillery practically nil, considerable enemy movement on back areas	
	11.10.17		Hostile 105 m.m. battery reported by aeroplane on second Church mound and then fired about 200 rounds at this target	
	12.10.17		Dull wet day. 62 Division relieved by the 3rd Division in artillery. 62 Division Artillery remaining in the line. S.O.R.A 3rd Divisional Artillery assumed command of the 62nd Divisional Artillery at 10 a.m.	
	13.10.17		Conditions normal	
	14.10.17		All quiet	
	15.10.17		Fired a barrage in support of a raid by 16th Division	
	16.10.17		All quiet	
	17.10.17		All quiet	
	18.10.17		All quiet	
	19.10.17		All quiet	Pkt

ORIGINAL

Army Form C. 2118.

WAR DIARY
or ʃ 312 Brigade R.F.A
INTELLIGENCE SUMMARY.
Sheet No 111

(Erase heading not required.)

Instructions regarding War Diaries and Intelligence Summaries are contained in F. S. Regs., Part II. and the Staff Manual respectively. Title pages will be prepared in manuscript.

Place	Date	Hour	Summary of Events and Information	Remarks and references to Appendices
1etten	20th 1917		All Quiet 2nd Lt ELLIS joined B/312 Bde for duty	
	21.10		All Quiet	
	22.10		All Quiet	
	23.10		All Quiet	
	24.10		On the night 24/25th 312 Bde RFA withdrew from the line to their wagon lines. 310 Bde RFA covering the whole sector	
	25.10		On the morning of the 25th the Brigade marched to new wagon lines x 6 b (ref. 51 C. S.F. 1:20000) on the evening of the same day the batteries relieved batteries of the 253 Bde RFA in the CHERISY Sector battery positions being taken up as follows A/312 N34 d 80 B/312 N34 d 45.65 C/312 N34 d 8 D32/42 86.65 ref. 51/B S.E. France 1:20000. The front covered extending from U 12. 6 5 K.O 14 a.9.4. and held by 51st Division. 152 Brigade on the left section, 15.2 Brigade on the right section	
	26.10		The command of the group passed from OC 29.3 Bde RFA to OC 312 Bde RFA at 4 pm under the direction of OC R.A. 51st R.A. JHL	

ORIGINAL

Army Form C. 2118.

WAR DIARY
of 312 Brigade RFA
Sheet No 10

INTELLIGENCE SUMMARY.
(Erase heading not required.)

Instructions regarding War Diaries and Intelligence Summaries are contained in F. S. Regs., Part II. and the Staff Manual respectively. Title pages will be prepared in manuscript.

Place	Date	Hour	Summary of Events and Information	Remarks and references to Appendices
October	27th	19.1	Batteries registered new targets and engaged the day's amount of movement observed in back area. The R.F.A. batteries on N34d were lightly shelled during the day.	
	28.10		Our batteries fired a feint barrage in support of a raid by the 49th Inf. Bde on our right. The raid was successful. On barrage duties the attention of the enemy away from the front attacked. Our batteries were heavily shelled by a 10.5 and 15.0 m.m. batteries during the day (one man killed.)	
	29.10		Our batteries were again rather severely shelled by a 15.0 m.m. battery and Lt-H Sutherland was killed when visiting the batteries in his capacity of signal officer (other ranks injured)	
	30.10		From 2 p.m. today 312 Bde RFA will cover the right section 51st Div.Arty front (FONTAINE) The 310 Bde RFA covering out the line and covering the Left section (CHERISY) Our batteries in N34d were again heavily shelled (15.0 m.m.) our	fff

ORIGINAL

Army Form C. 2118.

WAR DIARY
of 3/2 Brigade RFA
INTELLIGENCE SUMMARY. Sheet R.L.
(Erase heading not required.)

Place	Date	Hour	Summary of Events and Information	Remarks and references to Appendices
	October 30th 1918 2.10		Jun received a direct hit, not was put out of action. 34th Division relieved the 51st Division (less artillery) on the line 103 but 10be. Tempo over the right section, the 102 but 10be the left section. The bombardment of our batteries on N34d was rather less intense but B battery had one man killed and one gun put out of action	RHL

L. Olsby Lt. W. Hay.
Cmg 3/2 Bde RFA

Original

62nd D.

Vol II

War Diary

of

312th Brigade R.F.A.

Volume XI

From 1st November 1914
To 30th November 1914

ORIGINAL

Army Form C. 2118.

WAR DIARY
or of 312 Brigade R.F.A.
INTELLIGENCE SUMMARY.

(Erase heading not required.)

Instructions regarding War Diaries and Intelligence Summaries are contained in F. S. Regs., Part II. and the Staff Manual respectively. Title pages will be prepared in manuscript.

Place	Date	Hour	Summary of Events and Information	Remarks and references to Appendices
Avocourt	1/1/17		All quiet 2/Lt S.S. Lloyd appointed Signal Officer 312 Bde	
	2/1/17		Foggy all quiet	
	3/1/17		Thick fog all quiet one section B/312 moved to Hill 83 one section C/312 moved from Hill 288 to Hill 75.65	
	4/1/17		All quiet the remaining section of 312 Bde from Hill 258 to Hill 75.65	
	5/1/17		All quiet	
	6/1/17		Normal day, several fog	
	7/1/17		Misty day all quiet	
	8/1/17		S.O.S. from Hill 108 answered by C/312 Battery Harassing fire B/345 gms C/312 harassing fire station finished 9 pm Major J.R. Fleming left for a Battery commanders course in England, also for the relief of 62nd Divisional Artillery by 34th divisional artillery one section per Battery 312 Brigade relieved respectively, section of 152 Brigade R.F.A. Relief complete 9 pm.	RE

WAR DIARY
of 312 Brigade RFA
INTELLIGENCE SUMMARY
Sheet No II

Place	Date	Hour	Summary of Events and Information	Remarks and references to Appendices
November	11th 1914		Moved up. Quiet day. The relief of 312 Brigade RFA by 152 Brigade RFA completed at 9 pm. The command of the Group passed from A.Lt.Col. Tanks, 312 Bde RFA to A.Lt.Col. Thompson, 152 Bde RFA. The Brigade marched to BOIRY St MARTIN taking up a new position on road.	
	12/11/14		All guns and nineteen of the Brigade being in at dawn to No 27 Mobile workshop BAPAUME for overhaul. During the night the Brigade marched to new wagon lines in BEAURLENCOURT.	
	13/11/14		During the night the Brigade marched to new wagon lines on BAPASTE - company on the South side of the BAPASTE-ROCQUIGNY road.	
	14/11/14		Rest day. Lorry by.	
	15/11/14		Lorry day. All guns and nineteen brought in from BAPAUME to wagon lines.	JWL

ORIGINAL.

Army Form C. 2118.

WAR DIARY
or
INTELLIGENCE SUMMARY.

(Erase heading not required.)

of 7 Fd Bde RFA
Sheet No. III

Instructions regarding War Diaries and Intelligence Summaries are contained in F.S. Regs., Part II. and the Staff Manual respectively. Title pages will be prepared in manuscript.

Place	Date	Hour	Summary of Events and Information	Remarks and references to Appendices
November	15th 1917		Battery positions prepared on Q.1 (Reference map 1/20,000 sheet 57c NE and SE) and ammunition carried	
		16.11.17	to these positions as follows: 18 pounder 700 rounds per gun	
		17.11.17	4.5 howitzers 450 rounds per gun. The infantry secretly	
		18.11.17	kept practising all night long carrying out attack such	
	19.11.17		The Brigade marched at night. Guns were placed in position and laid, preparatory to the operation taking place. PGL [?] were prepared the following morning of the 20th as follows to Zero hour on the 20th the 62nd Division would attack HAVRINCOURT with two Brigades, about 185 Inf Bde. on the right, 187 Inf Bde. on the left. 186 Inf Bde. in reserve. 60 tanks were to proceed the infantry (were crushing and breaking the wire) (fighting tanks). These will advance under the barrage followed by the infantry. The following artillery will cover the	MK

T2134. Wt. W708—776. 500000. 4/15. Sir J. C. & S.

ORIGINAL

Army Form C. 2118.

WAR DIARY
or
INTELLIGENCE SUMMARY.

of J 3rd Bde signals M.7A
Aug to IV

(Erase heading not required.)

Place	Date	Hour	Summary of Events and Information	Remarks and references to Appendices
November	19th 1917		62nd Division 277th A.F.A., 93rd F.F.A., 163rd A.F.A., 310 & 77 A.F.A. 312 B.F.A. Brigades under the command of G.O.C.R.A. 62nd Div Arty. instructed by IV Corps.	
	20.11.17	6.20 am	The advance commenced. The 18 pounder creeping barrage lasting Zero to Zero + 2108 mn. and was entirely successful. The infantry advancing through HAVRINCOURT to a line running through 12.15 a & b central – 12.16 central 12.14 a & b central. The 186 Bde. then came into line and continued the advance. 312 Bde advanced at dawn to positions on 12.16 a. 12.14 a & front. A short barrage at 11.10 pm all quiet. 62nd Division to artillery relieved by 40th Division.	
	22.11.17			
	23.11.17	10.30 am	An advance by 20 Tanks and infantry attack was made on BOURLON. 312 Brigade managing into a large wood. 90 minutes. A considerable advance was made but BOURLON village was not taken.	M

ORIGINAL

Army Form C. 2118.

WAR DIARY
or
INTELLIGENCE SUMMARY.

(Erase heading not required.)

Army Form C. 2118.

Place	Date	Hour	Summary of Events and Information	Remarks and references to Appendices
Krumbu	23-24/11/17		During the night batteries replied to S.O.S. calls	
	24/11/17		All quiet	
	25/11/17		62nd Division relieved 40th Division on the line. G/RA 62nd Division relieved artillery taking over the command of the artillery Groups as follows. Right Group 5th RHA 74th RFA 181 RFA under Colol PALMER. Left Group 176 RFA 310 RFA 312 RFA under Colol PARSONS. Support Group covering 186 B.X. Bde. Left Regt. covering 187 Regt. Bde. General Relief 2nd IMABGS transferred 16RHA 2nd Cavalry Corps. Enemy shelling crucially increased. The bombardrs. 6/3/2 targets as follows Headquarters E29 a.1.1. A/3/2 E29 a.35.35. B/3/12 M10 b.44. C/312 B4.L.9.1. D/312 E29 d.20.25. At 6.20 am BOLLON village met again attacked & occupied by our artillery barrage. The village was carried by our troops & could not be held. The position became much the same as on the 25th inst.	

ORIGINAL

Army Form C. 2118.

WAR DIARY
or
INTELLIGENCE SUMMARY.

of 312 Brigade R.F.A. Sheet No ZT

(Erase heading not required.)

Instructions regarding War Diaries and Intelligence Summaries are contained in F. S. Regs., Part II. and the Staff Manual respectively. Title pages will be prepared in manuscript.

Place	Date	Hour	Summary of Events and Information	Remarks and references to Appendices
Havrincourt	27/11	10.12	2nd Lt. Linton, D. Battery wounded in the knee (slight)	
	28/11/17		Enemy shelling much more violent. Our batteries receiving considerable attention. 6.30am our batteries replied to an SOS call. 62nd Division on our right relieved by 47th Division in the line.	
	29/11/17		Enemy shelling considerable but mostly confined to roads and villages. 6.25am to 6.45am put down a barrage at a slow rate of fire in support of an infantry minor counter attack on the right flank.	
	30/11/17		At 9am the enemy put down a very heavy barrage. This was principally on roads and approaches to batteries, positions and villages and made it very difficult to replace Batteries. Answered the SOS call at 9am and continued to fire a barrage rate up to 10am when the trijets were withdrawn from the line to the south of HAVRINCOURT VILLAGE. MR	

ORIGINAL

Army Form C. 2118.

WAR DIARY
of 312 Brigade R.F.A.
INTELLIGENCE SUMMARY. Sheet No. VIII

(Erase heading not required.)

Instructions regarding War Diaries and Intelligence Summaries are contained in F. S. Regs., Part II. and the Staff Manual respectively. Title pages will be prepared in manuscript.

Place	Date	Hour	Summary of Events and Information	Remarks and references to Appendices
Inverness	30.9.1917		Casualties. The very severe barrage under which the batteries advanced to shorten the casualties to however were extremely light. 2 men being killed and 12 O.R's being cut. 10 men wounded. Two horses and two limbers were put out of action and others slightly damaged but first aid then soon found were all successfully withdrawn under heavy fire. The barrage put down by our guns appears to have been most effective, the enemy failing to bring any material advance.	MK

[signature]

Commanding 312 Brigade 13.7.A

Secret   Original

9/12

War Diary

of

312th Brigade, R.F.A.

Volume XII

From 1st December 1917
to 31st December 1917

ORIGINAL

Army Form C. 2118.

Instructions regarding War Diaries and Intelligence Summaries are contained in F. S. Regs., Part II. and the Staff Manual respectively. Title pages will be prepared in manuscript.

WAR DIARY
or of 312 Brigade R.F.A
INTELLIGENCE SUMMARY. Sheet No I
(Erase heading not required.)

Place	Date	Hour	Summary of Events and Information	Remarks and references to Appendices
	December 1st 1917		The Brigade moved into action at an early hour, batteries taking up positions in K.15.a. and thus able to bring enfilade fire to bear along the new F.14. All quiet. Another quiet day. The batteries put down a barrage barrage from 6.10pm. to 6.40pm. in support of a successful minor operation.	
	2.12.17			
	3.12.17		Destruction fire put down on several aeroplane calls. Enemy shelling all junctions of battery positions. All quiet at dusk. Batteries moved to new positions on K.39.a. section of batteries as follows A/312 K29.a.55.30 B/312 K.39.a.45.50 C/312 K29.a.0.2 D/312 K29.a.93. Brigade Headquarters Farm heated on dugout K.35.c.4.4.Y	
	4.12.17		The 47th Division were withdrawn from the BOURLON position to the HINDENBURGH SUPPORT line. The factory GRAINCOURT – LA JUSTICE being held by 119th Infantry Brigade, who cover the withdrawal and evacuation of the	

T.131. Wt. W708–776. 500000. 4/15. Sir J. C. & S.

Army Form C. 2118.

WAR DIARY
or of 312 Brigade R.F.A
INTELLIGENCE SUMMARY.
Sheet No. 2.

(Erase heading not required.)

Place	Date	Hour	Summary of Events and Information	Remarks and references to Appendices
December	4th 1917		Main line. This was carried out without incident	
	5.12.17		Very quiet day. The outpost line was withdrawn at dusk to the main line. The artillery putting down a evening fire to assist the withdrawal and consolidation	
	6.12.17		Foggy day, all quiet	
	7.12.17		All quiet	
	8.12.17		All quiet	
	9.12.17		8am answered S.O.S call, later considerable enemy movement was observed. D/312 battery silenced an enemy 6 gun 10.5 m.m. battery which came into action on the front	
	10.12.17		2.30 am batteries replied to a S.O.S call. D/312 engaged active enemy and cleared the detachments. A quiet day. All quiet	
	11.12.17			
	12.12.17		235 Bde R.F.A relieved 312 Bde R.F.A who in turn relieved 153 Bde R.F.A. The relief being complete at 4 p.m. Batteries of 312 Bde R.F.A taking up positions in J30d (France 57c 1/40,000)	PAS

ORIGINAL

Army Form C. 2118.

WAR DIARY
or
of 312 Brigade R.F.A
INTELLIGENCE SUMMARY.
(Erase heading not required.) Sheet No. 3.

Place	Date	Hour	Summary of Events and Information	Remarks and references to Appendices
Hebuterne	12th 1917		Headquarters being situated in Quarry T.36.a.1.9.	
	13/12/17		Prisoners captured on the night of the 12th gave information of an intended attack at 6.30am on the 13th Batteries fired a barrage on enemy front line trenches from 6 am to 40 am and the attack if intended did not materialise. At 8.30am & 8.35 am Batteries assisted in our artillery concentration on RAINCOURT. The reinforcement Officers definitely posted 2/Lt DOWLE to N/312 2nd Lt DOROTHERN to B/312 2nd Lt FEDDES to C/312 N/312 2nd Lt EABAR to D.312.	
	14.12.17		That 7/ all quiet.	
	15/12/17		All quiet 2nd Lieut ARTHUR evacuated sick to England	
	16.12.17		All quiet. Frost and slight fall of snow	
	17/12/17		All quiet frost continues	
	18/12/17		Slight shelling of Battery positions	
	19/12/17		All quiet. Very contains	
	20.12.17		All Frost. V.5.	JWL

ORIGINAL

Army Form C. 2118.

WAR DIARY
or
INTELLIGENCE SUMMARY.
(Erase heading not required.)

Instructions regarding War Diaries and Intelligence
Summaries are contained in F. S. Regs., Part II.
and the Staff Manual respectively. Title pages
will be prepared in manuscript.

Place	Date	Hour	Summary of Events and Information	Remarks and references to Appendices
December	21.12.14		All quiet, frost continues	
	22.12.14		All quiet, frost continues	
	23.12.14		All quiet, frost continues	
	24.12.14		Slight shelling of battery positions, snow and slight thaw	
	25.12.14		All quiet, fine day, still thaw	
	26.12.14		The Brigade withdrawn to the wagon lines, the batteries being all clear at 3 p.m. Orders received that the Brigade would march to COURCELLES LE COMTE on the morning of the 27th inst.	
	27.12.14		Owing to frost the march was cancelled	
	28.12.14		The Brigade marched at 10.45 a.m. to COURCELLES	
	29.12.14		The Brigade marched at 9.30 a.m. to HARTEVILLE and occupied billets in the village. H.EDWARDS commn. ticn b. hree	
	30.12.14		The Brigade marched at 11.45 a.m. to Wagon Lines at LA TARGETTE (Sheet France 5-13 1:40000)	
	31.12.14		All guns and howitzers sent in to workshop for overhaul	

F.A.Arnold-Forster, Major
Commanding 3/2 Bde R.F.A

SECRET

Confidential

312

Brigade RFA

WAR DIARY

ORIGINAL

Volume XIII

From 1st January 1918
To 31st January 1918.

ORIGINAL

WAR DIARY of 7 312 Bde BTA

Army Form C. 2118.

INTELLIGENCE SUMMARY. Sheet No 1

Place	Date	Hour	Summary of Events and Information	Remarks and references to Appendices
January	1st 1918		The following Officers, NCO's and men received decorations in New Year's Honours list and for Gallantry during the operations commenced on 20th November on the CAMBRAI front: New Year Honours Major Bruce FORSTER D.S.O. to 78612/ Serjt WHITTAKER DCM. CAMBRAI Offensive Lt J.B. BODEN M.C. and Bar. 2nd Lt. RC Turton M.C. 2nd Lt F.T. WILLIAMS M.C. No 785526 B.S.M. BOWDEN M.C. No 686744 Cpl. JEFFERY D.C.M. No 785246 Sjt HEBBLETHWAITE R.A. No 686744 Sgt BLACK R.A. No 82908 Sgt YATES R.A. No 786045 Sgt LITTLEWELL R.A. No 78621 Lgt. HIRTH R.A. No 786591 Bdr BEARS No 785656 Bdr DAVIES A.A. No 68743 Bdr EMMETT R.A. No 786414 Cpl WORSNOP R.A. No 686742 Sr/Bdr POTTS R.A. No 685597 S/2 HASLAM R.A. No 786146 P. HOBBS R.A. No 786216 S/2 HEATEN R.A. No 746419 P. FRENCH R.A. No 786344 S/2 CLAYTON R.A. No 786264 S/S WITTHAM R.A. No 786010 Driver PARKINSON A.A. No 856b6 Dr SLATER R.A. No 840349/ Pt YATES/ R.A.M.C. No 1899RLM BUTCHER R.M. No 496257 Sgt FISHER R.A. No 954 250 Pt STANDING R.A.	HL

ORIGINAL

Army Form C. 2118.

WAR DIARY
or *of 312 Brigade RFA*
INTELLIGENCE SUMMARY. *Sheet No II*

(Erase heading not required.)

Instructions regarding War Diaries and Intelligence Summaries are contained in F. S. Regs., Part II. and the Staff Manual respectively. Title pages will be prepared in manuscript.

Place	Date	Hour	Summary of Events and Information	Remarks and references to Appendices
January	2nd 1919		The Brigade remained in rest at LA TARGETTE	9th
	3rd			
	4th			
	5th		Relets presented by G.O.C. 1st Army to a Bombardier, Driver & 2 Gunners of the Brigade in respect of devotion to gallantry during the CAMBRAI Offensive	9th
	6th			
	7th			
	8th			
	9th		The Brigade remained in rest at LA TARGETTE	9th
	10th			
	11th			
	12th			
	13th			
	14th		Section of Batteries 312 Brigade RFA relieved corresponding sections of 281 Brigade RFA on the ORRY Sector	9th
	15th		The relief of 281 Brigade by 312 Brigade completed the	9th / 9th

ORIGINAL

WAR DIARY
of 312 Brigade RFA
INTELLIGENCE SUMMARY.
Sheet No. III

Army Form C. 2118.

Place	Date	Hour	Summary of Events and Information	Remarks and references to Appendices
	January	15th Feb/18	Command of the Group passed from Lt.Col. Rothwell DSO to Lt.Col. Edmeades 8pm. The 62nd Divisional Artillery covering the 62nd Division on the line being grouped as follows. Right Group 310 Brigade RFA covering the FAVREUIL sector Left Group 312 Brigade RFA covering the SAPPY sector.	
		16th	All Quiet. Battery positions are as follows A/312 4 guns B26 d 4.3.51. 2 guns B15 c 0.4.62, B/312 4 guns B26 b 6.3.35. 2 guns B21 b 9.2.37. Tanks Sect. B17 c 8.6. C/312 4 guns B26 a 4.4.41. 2 guns B21 b 9.2.40, D/312 4 guns B26 b 8 6.07. 2 guns B21 b 9.6.53 Reference Map France 1:10000 51B N.W.	9PL
		17th	All Quiet. Ammunition allowance 125 rounds per day for 18pndr. Batteries 60 rounds per day 4.5" Howitzer Battery this ammunition being mostly expended on sniping enemy morning harassing fire.	9PL
		18th	All Quiet	9PL
		19th	All Quiet	9PL 9PL

ORIGINAL

Army Form C. 2118.

WAR DIARY
of 3/2 Brigade R.F.A.
INTELLIGENCE SUMMARY.
(Erase heading not required.)

Instructions regarding War Diaries and Intelligence Summaries are contained in F. S. Regs., Part II. and the Staff Manual respectively. Title pages will be prepared in manuscript.

Sheet No. IV

Place	Date	Hour	Summary of Events and Information	Remarks and references to Appendices
January	26th	1512	All quiet, thick fog	144
	21st		All quiet, thick general mist	144
	22nd		All quiet. Brig: M.R.H. CROFTON DSO 72TH posted to C/312	144
	23rd			
	24th		All quiet. Misty and foggy weather	144
	25th			
	26th			
	27th		All quiet. Scond: (A/Capt) H.E. SHARP posted to England	144
	28th		All quiet, thick mist	144
	29th		2nd Lt. T.T. WILLIAMS D/312 posted to 62nd DAC. Lt. S.A. BISHOP from 62nd DAC posted to C/312	144
	30th		10pm to 10.15 pm heavy concentration of enemy trench mortar fire on our front line trenches. In attack Howard Battery of Group retaliated with a concentration from 10.25 pm to 10.35 pm on enemy trenches round OPPY WOOD	144

ORIGINAL

Army Form C. 2118.

WAR DIARY
or ~~INTELLIGENCE SUMMARY~~
of 3/2 Brigade RFA Sheet No. V

(Erase heading not required.)

Instructions regarding War Diaries and Intelligence Summaries are contained in F. S. Regs., Part II. and the Staff Manual respectively. Title pages will be prepared in manuscript.

Place	Date	Hour	Summary of Events and Information	Remarks and references to Appendices
January	31st 1916		Another day of thick fog. 7.50pm & 9.55pm batteries replied to S.O.S call for support by the 31st Division on the Left.	AH

W. Falon
Lt. Col.
Commanding 3/2 Brigade RFA

Original.

SECRET

312

Brigade RFA

War Diary

ORIGINAL

Volume XIV

From 1st. Feb. 1918.
To. 28th. Feb. 1918.

WAR DIARY of 92 Brigade RHA
INTELLIGENCE SUMMARY.
(Erase heading not required.) Sheet No 1

Army Form C. 2118.

Instructions regarding War Diaries and Intelligence Summaries are contained in F. S. Regs., Part II. and the Staff Manual respectively. Title pages will be prepared in manuscript.

Place	Date	Hour	Summary of Events and Information	Remarks and references to Appendices
In the Field	February 1st 1918		All quiet	JHL
	2nd		All quiet	JHL
	3rd		Hostile artillery more active. Snipers posted to B/312 battery	JHL
	4th		Enemy artillery again more active. BAILEUL receiving considerable attention. 2nd Lt T. Donovan (SR) joined the Brigade, posted to A/312 battery	JHL
	5th		Enemy artillery and our own heavy batteries very active	JHL
	6th		All quiet	JHL
	7th		All quiet	JHL
	8th		Enemy artillery active on our batteries/positions in BAILLEUL	JHL
	9th		— on BAILLEUL. We find no enemy front line in retaliation	JHL
	10th		BAILLEUL again heavily shelled. Enemy artillery active, particularly between 2 PM and 10 PM on Brie & Bund	JHL
	11th		All quiet	JHL
	12th		All quiet	JHL

WAR DIARY
or
INTELLIGENCE SUMMARY

Army Form C. 2118.

312th Brigade R.F.A. Sheet 2

Place	Date	Hour	Summary of Events and Information	Remarks and references to Appendices
February	13	9/15	Some Lull shelling of battery positions	B.12
	14		All quiet	9/14
	15		Forward sections & Tank farm relieved by correspondence batteries of 281 Brigade, Completed by midnight	B.13 B.13
	#15		Batty./B./I.M.WHITWORTH reported for duty & took to D. Battery	B.13
	16		Relief completed by 281 Brigade at 19 noon when command passed. Batteries handed over, turns right & took over those of 26, 132 Btys on rest area. Batteries billeted & horses at following places	
			A/ SAVY B/D CAUCOURT C/ FREVIN CAPEL H.Q. at MAISON ROYEE, AUBIGNY	
			When H.Q. Battys & leaving H.Q. for ARRAS-BAILLEUL Rd, billets on the road were heavily shelled by not yet for an hour.	E.14
	17/19		In rest. E.H.Q. Reserve	B.14 B.15
	20		Capt. CLAYTON BARKER reported for duty	B.13
	21/22			B.14
	23		Lt TANNER reported for duty & posted to A BATTERY	B.15

(Original)

WAR DIARY of 312 Brigade RFA
INTELLIGENCE SUMMARY.
(Erase heading not required.)

Army Form C. 2118.

Sheet No. 3

Instructions regarding War Diaries and Intelligence Summaries are contained in F. S. Regs., Part II. and the Staff Manual respectively. Title pages will be prepared in manuscript.

Place	Date	Hour	Summary of Events and Information	Remarks and references to Appendices
February	24th 1918		The Brigade remained at rest in G.H.Q. reserve	
	25th			
	26th			
	27th			
	28th			

[signature]
Lt. Col. Commanding
312 Brigade RFA

62nd Divisional Artillery

WAR DIARY

312th BRIGADE R. F. A.

MARCH 1918

62nd

Vol 15
Original

(6339) Wt. W160/M3016 1,500,000 10/17 McA & W Ltd (E1898) Forms W3091.   Army Form W.3091.

Cover for Documents.

Nature of Enclosures.

WAR DIARY.

312TH BRIGADE R.F.A.

VOL XV

Notes, or Letters written.

WAR DIARY
of 312 Brigade R.F.A
INTELLIGENCE SUMMARY. Sheet No. I ORIGINAL
(Erase heading not required.)

Army Form C. 2118.

Place	Date	Hour	Summary of Events and Information	Remarks and references to Appendices
	March 1st 1918		312 Brigade remain in G.H.Q reserve	Appx
	2nd		do	Appx
	3rd		do	Appx
	4th		do	Appx
	5th		One section per battery 312 Brigade R.F.A relieved one section per battery 170th Brigade R.F.A 31st Divisional Artillery	Appx
	6th		The relief of 170th Brigade by 312 Brigade R.F.A completed; personnel only were relieved from Brigade H.Q being rather older. The situation is as follows 310 Brigade R.F.A (Right Group) covers 184 Infantry Brigade, 62nd Division ARLEUX sector. 312 Brigade R.F.A (Left Group) covers 186 Infantry Brigade in the line ACHEVILLE sector. 312 Brigade R.F.A Forester as Follows. Reference Map France 51 B.N.W. and 36 c SW. Headquarters B.8.a.3.0. A/312 B1.d.9.5 B/312 B3.y.a.8.2. C/312 T19.c.5.5. D/312 T26.d.9.3. Two tank guns are at T29.a.3.9 and at T22.d.15.80. Command of Left Group passed to Lt Col A.C. EDEN 9am	Appx Appx Appx Appx
	7th		all quiet	Appx
	8th		all quiet all day	Appx
	9th		all quiet	Appx
	10th		all quiet	Appx
	11th		all quiet	Appx
	12th		all quiet	Appx

WAR DIARY
or
INTELLIGENCE SUMMARY.

of 6/312 Brigade RFA Sheet No. 2 ORIGINAL

Army Form C. 2118.

Place	Date	Hour	Summary of Events and Information	Remarks and references to Appendices
March	13th	1918	In anticipation of an enemy attack on this front all troops ordered to stand to from 5 a.m. to daylight. Quiet day, normal harassing fire at night	9/1
	14th		All quiet—	14/1
	15th		B/312 RFA bombed with a barrage a raid made by the Canadians on our left. Raid successful. 15 prisoners taken	14/1
	16th		all quiet—	14/1
	17th		Our infantry successfully raided the enemy trenches at 11 p.m. on Lattorre giving artillery support	14/1
	18th		all quiet. wet day	14/1
	19th		all quiet— wet day	14/1
	20th		All quiet (below normal)	14/1
	21st		From 5 a.m. to 9 a.m. heavy artillery bombardment of our Lattorre, 7AB, B+C, WIKKERVAL, 72B, 27 B2, 3, 8 + 9 all calibres Yellow × Gas (mustard) also used. Enemy quiet from 4:30 am to 11 am a rather less violent bombardment than on the previous day. evening all quiet	9/1
	22nd		A/312 and B/312 relieved in the line by 24th and 30th batteries Canadian FA and marched to wagon lines.	14/1
	23rd		5.15 a.m. to 5.25 a.m. fired S.O.S. 9 a.m. A/312 and B/312 marched from wagon lines to a position of readiness on M10 Reference Map FRANCE 5/B 1:40000. Headquarters remaining in action with a group	

Army Form C. 2118.

WAR DIARY
or
INTELLIGENCE SUMMARY.
(Erase heading not required.)

[of] 312 Brigade R.F.A.

Pl. & L. 3. 0218/1946.

Instructions regarding War Diaries and Intelligence Summaries are contained in F. S. Regs., Part II. and the Staff Manual respectively. Title pages will be prepared in manuscript.

Place	Date	Hour	Summary of Events and Information	Remarks and references to Appendices
March	24th (cont)		Covering of 30th Battery C/74. 30th Battery C/74. C/312 and D/312 every one's day. At 11.30 pm Headquarters, C/312 and D/312 withdrew to Wagon Lines.	
	25th	At 8 am	Headquarters, C/312 and D/312 marched to AYETTE. A/312 and B/312 from the column at BOIRY ST RICTRUDE. Ordered to push on to BUCQUOY from there to MONCHY AU BOIS and thence to HANNESCAMPS, batteries taking up positions on E.18.d and E.23.b at 10 pm Reference Map FRANCE 5Y.D. 1:40,000	ML
	26th		Brigade headquarters remained at HANNESCAMPS, batteries in action, with wagon supply, team kept up close to the guns - a quiet day	ML
	27th		3/2 Brigade R.F.A. are in Colonel CARDEW's Group "Left Group" 622nd Divisional Artillery covering 185 Infantry Brigade. Group consists of 190th Bde. 1/187 Bde, 93rd Bde, 312 Bde. Batteries fired during the day dispersing all attempts of the enemy to mass for attack and at night answered S.O.S calls	ML
	28th	12.44 pm	Brigade headquarters moved up to Depart at E.24.a.2.5 fired S.O.S 1.35 pm fired S.O.S 2.35 and 3.25 pm. A/312, B/312 MONTGOMERY and D/312 MIOSFORD arranged night guilt considerable enemy movement within range of guns. There was engaged with good effect. All quiet.	ML
	29th			ML

(A7092). Wt. W12859/M1293. 75,000. 1/17. D. D. & L., Ltd. Forms/C.2118 14.

Army Form C. 2118.

WAR DIARY
of 312 Brigade R.F.A.
INTELLIGENCE SUMMARY.
Sheet No. 4. Original

(Erase heading not required.)

Instructions regarding War Diaries and Intelligence Summaries are contained in F. S. Regs., Part II. and the Staff Manual respectively. Title pages will be prepared in manuscript.

Place	Date	Hour	Summary of Events and Information	Remarks and references to Appendices
Acheux	30th	1918	Enemy batteries, wagon lines and minor movement engaged with effect. Hostile shelling quiet. Hot dry.	
	31st		Another quiet day	

R. Bellew
Lt Col
Commanding 312 Brigade R.F.A.

62nd Divisional Artillery

WAR DIARY

312th BRIGADE

ROYAL FIELD ARTILLERY

APRIL 1918

Original.   Confidential

War Diary

of

312th Brigade R.F.A.

Volume F/16

From 1st April 1918
To 30th April 1918

WAR DIARY
of 3/2 Brigade RFA
INTELLIGENCE SUMMARY

Army Form C. 2118.

Phase No 1   ORIGINAL

Place	Date	Hour	Summary of Events and Information	Remarks and references to Appendices
April	10th	1918	Enemy battery engaged out silence on K.21.d. Movement seen by forward O.P. in R.21.a bright until 8 effing Bois D. fire pendant on PHUSIEUX at 10.50pm 12.15am and 1.45am Enemy artillery quiet less movement observed. Enemy artillery more active about 100 rounds 105 2pm. How fell near battery position.	JKL
	22nd		4.50am to 5.5am Intense Enemy 6 inch & 10.5 preparation found on hostile regt. shoots down to 500 yards Enemy artillery normal.	JKL
	23rd		Point J. WILLEY A battery 3/2 Brigade RFA killed in the forward OP. Considerable movement of troops and transport observed out of range of field guns. Reported that by enemy artillery on batteries	JKL
	4th		in the Northern outskirts of EZNARTS	
	5th		5.30am to 6 & 2am batteries 3/2 Bde RFA fired a creeping barrage in support of an attack by 63rd Infantry Brigade and 4th Australian Infantry Brigade on ROSSIGNOL WOOD and the Sunken Road. Enemy retaliation 8.30am k.18.30am and hostile fire enemy 103 12.59pm .105 on L.6.8 between 12.20pm to 12.50pm fire on L.8.C and 2.Cd 1.6pm an battery engaged. Enemy shrapnel on L.8.C and 2.Cd 1.6pm an battery ranged fire. Enemy 105 in L.8 central. 2.40pm D/32 battery engaged and silenced enemy battery at L.16.a.3.2 and L.22.a.5.9 3.35pm to 4.36pm fired all batteries on L.13 line as a plan fire to cover our attack to regain ground lost in BUCQUOY	JKL

WAR DIARY

or INTELLIGENCE SUMMARY

Army Form C. 2118.

of 3/12 Brigade RFA
Sheet No. 2

Place	Date	Hour	Summary of Events and Information	Remarks and references to Appendices
April	5th 1918		Continued 1.14 am to 1.30 pm fired S.18 crossing the bottom part of MIRAUMONT from a column by the enemy. 5.15 am to 11 am the enemy put down a very heavy bombardment of all calibre, 150 m.m., 10.5 m.m, 18 pounders & 4.1 in., a very large proportion being gas shell on battery position, mostly on T.15.b.17, b.18, b.23, b.24, PIGEON WOOD, F.NARTS, PIGEON WOOD and on front line trenches. Battery replied with heavy counter battery on enemy land front Guns. The following Lieutenants attended school Cont's Major CROFTON R.S.O. Captain SENIOR, Lt BODEN M.C., Lt NISSIM, 2nd Lt STUTTLE, 2nd Lt PATTOCK all of C battery and 10 N.C.O's and men.	AA
	6th		5 am to 5.15 am all batteries except C/3/12 on pen in a storm fired counter preparation. batch artillery normal	M
	7th		4.30 am to 5 am all batteries fired on S.O.S. line at a slow rate. 10 am to 11 pm enemy put down a destructive shoot on B/3/12 only slight damage done to gun (no direct hits) Major BRADFORD and Lt BROTHERS (from 2/3/12) Major TUTHILL Lt NICHOLSON (from 5/3/12) Lt HATCHER to A/3/12, and Captain CLAYTON, BARKER DCM posted to C/3/12 (from A/3/12)	M

INTELLIGENCE SUMMARY

of 312 Brigade R.F.A. Sheet No. 8

(Erase heading not required.)

072/8/1/NAL

Instructions regarding War Diaries and Intelligence Summaries are contained in F. S. Regs., Part II and the Staff Manual respectively. Title pages will be prepared in manuscript.

Place	Date	Hour	Summary of Events and Information	Remarks and references to Appendices
April	8/4	8/4	Quiet day. hostile artillery normal	1 At
	9th		Quiet day. low visibility	1 At
	10th		Quiet day. hostile artillery normal	1 At
	11th		Counter Preparation fired at 5am and 2am	1 At
	12th		Quiet day, hostile artillery normal. From 6pm 62nd Division artillery relieved by that of "Major Group". 312 Bde R.F.A. 210 Bde R.F.A, 211 Bde R.F.A covering 185 Infantry brigade. "Left Group". 295 Bde R.F.A, 296 Bde R.F.A, 26 SA Bde R.F.A covering 186 Infantry brigade	1 At
	13th		Quiet day. wet.	1 At
	14th		Quiet day. hostile artillery normal	1 At
	15th		hostile artillery active. Battery positions receiving considerable attention at dusk. One 5.9in C/342 and one howitzer D/812 proved to a forward position at F19d30	1 At
	16th		Counter Preparation fired at 4.30am and 6.45am considerable enemy movement seen and engaged. wet night	9 At
	17th		Counter Preparation fired at 2am. Dont Freuna Kronbga carried out destruction shots on enemy batteries with excellent results. Movement in back area impeded by the frequent position of enemy Kronbga's. Concentration shoots on batteries at 5 & 5:1pm shewed to cause the enemy heavy casualties	9 At

Army Form C. 2118.

INTELLIGENCE SUMMARY.

of 17 312 Brigade RFA

Sheet No 4 07/8/1144

(Erase heading not required.)

Place	Date	Hour	Summary of Events and Information	Remarks and references to Appendices
April	18th	19/8	Counter Preparation fire at 4.55 AM wet and quiet during day. Bde Group "C" 62nd Division Artillery now consists of 187th Bde RFA, 310th Bde RFA and 312th Bde RFA under the command of Lt Col. SHERLOCK D.S.O. Counter Preparation fired at 5.55 am for 5 minutes	JHL
	19th			JHL
	20th		All quiet. Command & movements seen and engaged with effect.	JHL
	21st		Command of "Right Group" passed to Lt Col A.G. EDEN 312 Brigade RFA at 18 am. D/312 engaged and silenced two active enemy batteries	JHL
	22nd		Another quiet day at 8.45 pm 200 rounds 4.5" Howitzer Little shell fired into Senkern Road I.8.d.	JHL
	23rd		187th Infantry brigade relieved on the line by 63rd Infantry Brigade at the same time 42nd Division relieved then front to I.2.c.9.1. at 6 pm 187th Brigade RFA were withdrawn into Corps Reserve. Brigt Genl then consisting of 310 Bde RFA and 312th Bde RFA covering 63rd Inf Bde	JHL
	24th		Another quiet day. Major TATHILL O/312 and Lt H COCKERELL B/312 evacuated wounded C.R.S. 2nd Lt W Ric E. EAGAR D/312 appointed orderly officer 312 Brigade RFA	JHL

(A7092). Wt. W12859/M1293. 75,000. 1/17. D. D. & L., Ltd. Forms/C.2118 14.

INTELLIGENCE SUMMARY

Army Form C. 2118

No. of Brigade: 312 Brigade R.F.A.

Ref. No. S- 072181/AK

Instructions regarding War Diaries and Intelligence Summaries are contained in F. S. Regs., Part II. and the Staff Manual respectively. Title pages will be prepared in manuscript.

(Erase heading not required.)

Place	Date	Hour	Summary of Events and Information	Remarks and references to Appendices
April	25th	1918	Orders received at 4.10am. Personnel of 62nd Division Artillery to take over from us the "Centre Sector" on the 25th and 26th Inst. On the same date personnel of 39th Div. Arty. to take over from 62nd Division in the left sector. One section per battery exchanged personnel, the relief being complete at 4pm. 123rd Bde R.F.A. relieving 310th Bde R.F.A. and 124th Bde R.F.A. relieving 312th Bde R.F.A.	J.McL
	26th		The remaining two sections per battery exchanged reliefs complete at 4.30am. The command of the Right Group at the same time passed to O.C. 312 Brigade R.F.A. Headquarters at SOUASTRE. Batteries withdrew to rest billets at SOUASTRE. Command of 310 Bde R.F.A. and 312 Bde R.F.A. coming under the Command of Lieut-Col SHERLOCK D.S.O. with Headquarters at CHATEAU DE LA HAIE J.6. Reference Map 51D.N.E 1.20.000	J.McL
	27th		Headquarters 312 Brigade R.F.A. remained at rest in SOUASTRE	J.McL

Lt Col
Commanding 312 Brigade R.F.A.

SECRET ORIGINAL

95/17

312 BRIGADE RFA

WAR DIARY

ORIGINAL

Volume XVII

From 1st May 1918
To 31st May 1918

WAR DIARY of 312 Brigade RFA

ORIGINAL — Army Form C. 2118
INTELLIGENCE SUMMARY. Sheet No 1.

Place	Date	Hour	Summary of Events and Information	Remarks and references to Appendices
	1st	19.8	B Brigade headquarters in Rest Billets in SOUSTRE	
	2nd		At 12 noon Brigade Headquarters moved to Jba 6.3 near CHATEAU DE LA HAIE. Reference map 51/3 N.E. 1:20,000 taking over from Lt Col SHERLOCK D.S.O. commanding 306 Brigade RFA and 312 Brigade RFA "Right Group" of 42nd Divisional Artillery covering 42nd Division in the line. Canadian Division IVth Corps front	JAL
	3rd		Batteries are located as follows A30 (4 guns) K16.54.20 (2 guns) K14.v3.40 B30 (6 guns) V2c.2.v.32 B30(6 gms) J2A.V.63 B310(6 Hows) V1a 31.20. A31.2(6 guns) V3a 22.23. B31.2(6 guns) V1a 09.91. B31.2(6 guns) K.A. 22.60.) J31.2 (4 Hows) J12 & 9.28 (2 hows) K2c 24.24. A quiet day.	JAL
	4th		Batteries fired a barrage in support of an infantry attack on the Sunken Advancing road and Arleux loop and line from the light front. The attack was successful all objectives were made and retained from line now unapproximately down K1a 00 to J3a 45.40	JAL JAL JAL
	5th		All quiet, wet day	JAL
	6th		All quiet 42nd Division relieved in the line by 5yth Division	JAL
	7th		All quiet	
8th to 14th		Headquarters 312 Brigade RFA relieved by Headquarters 308 Brigade RFA on the 8th. 312 Brigade proceeded by march route to billets AUTHIE at 12 noon	JAL

Army Form C. 2118.

WAR DIARY
or
INTELLIGENCE SUMMARY.

(Erase heading not required.)   Sheet No 2   ORIGINAL

of 312 Brigade RFA

Instructions regarding War Diaries and Intelligence Summaries are contained in F. S. Regs., Part II. and the Staff Manual respectively. Title pages will be prepared in manuscript.

Place	Date	Hour	Summary of Events and Information	Remarks and references to Appendices
War	14th	10/8	312 Brigade RFA (Lt Col. EDEN) relieved 310 Brigade RFA (Lt Col. SHERLOCK) headquarters in line at 12 noon. From 9am to 12.30pm downing of "Right Grouls" awaitie in gas bombardment of STAR WOOD, LA LOUVIERE FARM and /u200	JAL
	15th		All quiet, all 11 pm enemy sent up gas rockets in the direction of Valley No.	JAL
	16		10 am hostile bombardment of our front and support line known	JAL
			10.25 am to 10.35 pm all available batteries concentrated on enemy bottom machine gun nest and enemy trench	JAL
	17th		All quiet 10.30 pm Shantyn but observe a gas concentration on Box Wood	JAL
	18th		All quiet fine day	JAL
	19th		All quiet fine day	JAL
	20th		All quiet fine day	JAL
	21st		All quiet. 312 Brigade RFA relieved by headquarters 310 Brigade RFA. 312 Brigade RFA headquarters moved to new billets at AUTHIE	JAL
	21st to 29th		headquarters remained in new billets at AUTHIE.	JAL

Army Form C. 2118.

WAR DIARY
of 312 Brigade R.F.A.
INTELLIGENCE SUMMARY.
(Erase heading not required.) Sheet No. 3. ORIGINAL

Instructions regarding War Diaries and Intelligence Summaries are contained in F. S. Regs., Part II. and the Staff Manual respectively. Title pages will be prepared in manuscript.

Place	Date	Hour	Summary of Events and Information	Remarks and references to Appendices
May	29th	19.8	312 Brigade R.F.A. headquarters relieved 310 Brigade on the line at 12 noon.	ppl. ppl. ppl.
	30th		All quiet this day. Enemy artillery more active.	
	31st		Fine though day. Enemy artillery again active.	

W. Allen
Lt Col
Commanding 312 Brigade R.F.A.

SECRET

Vol 18

312 BRIGADE R.F.A.

WAR DIARY.

ORIGINAL

Volume XVIII

From 1st June 1918 to 30th June 1918.

Army Form C. 2118.

WAR DIARY
or
of 312 Brigade RFA
INTELLIGENCE SUMMARY. Sheet No. I   ORIGINAL

(Erase heading not required.)

Instructions regarding War Diaries and Intelligence
Summaries are contained in F. S. Regs., Part II.
and the Staff Manual respectively. Title pages
will be prepared in manuscript.

Place	Date	Hour	Summary of Events and Information	Remarks and references to Appendices
	June 1st 1916	3.25 Am	A heavy barrage came down on our front and support line Trenches. 3.30 Am SOS signals went up along the whole M.Gye. front. Artillery opened at once and continued to fire as S.O.S. lines until 4 am. Stray rifle & rapid fire was reported from advanced trenches all am. Enemy retaliated & put a strong hot artillery fire on front	1st
	2nd		All quiet. Fine day. C battery practice silencer ammunition. No firing. Fine and still	1st
	3rd		Moderate fire from enemy artillery	1st
	4th		C battery open shelled	1st / 2nd
	5th		Artillery again successful attention from enemy artillery Headquarters 312 Brigade RFA relieved on the line by Headquarters 310 Brigade RFA	1st / 2nd
	7th / 10th		Headquarters remained in rest at ARTAIZE	1st / 2nd

WAR DIARY
INTELLIGENCE SUMMARY

Army Form C. 2118.

of 312 Brigade R.F.A.   ORIGINAL
Month of 2

Place	Date	Hour	Summary of Events and Information	Remarks and references to Appendices
France	11th 1918		Batteries 312 Brigade R.F.A. withdrawn from the line & their horses taken. The Brigade now being in "Corps Reserve" ordered 2 hours notice to move. One section of M/312 placed in BAYENCOURT to act as mobile "Anti Tank Section" for Centre Division.	JHL
	12th 15th 18th		The Brigade remained at Mezeres bois in "CORPS RESERVE"	JHL
	18th		312 Brigade R.F.A. relieved 295 Brigade R.F.A. in the line. Becoming "Z" (Reffer-Froch) Left Divisional Artillery. Covering 186 Infantry Brigade. Brigade H.Q and Batteries are treated as follows. Reference Map Sheet 57D N.E.	JHL
	19th		Headquarters E23c 5.5 A/312 2gun action E24a 3.7 4 guns silent E16d 5.5 B/312 2gun action E28b 7.9 4 gun silent E22b 2.7 Anti Tank gun 15 November F26a 2.2 C/312 action from (1) F19d 3.0 (3) E23b 70.25 D/312 action from (1) F19d 3.0 (5) E18c 35-48. All quiet.	JHL
	20th 21st		All quiet-fired some artillery to mark movement of Tanks. Hostile artillery more active. Fired noise barrage from 10.30 to 10.50 pm.	JHL JHL

Army Form C. 2118.

WAR DIARY
or
INTELLIGENCE SUMMARY.

of 312 Brigade R.F.A. Sheet No. 3

ORIGINAL

(Erase heading not required.)

Place	Date	Hour	Summary of Events and Information	Remarks and references to Appendices
France	22nd	14/18	Headquarters and C Battery again shelled. From 11.27pm to 2am active gun fired a barrage in support of an infantry raid supported by 5 tanks. The raid was not successful being unable to advance owing to heavy machine gun fire. Enemy artillery again active.	A/K A/L G/L
	23			
	24		One section per battery relieved by section of 124 Bde R.F.A. In the early morning between guns fired annihilating fire.	
	25		The relief of 312 Bde R.F.A. by 124 Bde R.F.A. completed by 10 pm.	A/K
	26		312 Bde R.F.A. marching to ORVILLE.	
	to 30		The Brigade remained in billets in ORVILLE being in GHQ reserve and also at the disposal of IV Corps for the purpose of reinforcing other front.	G/L

W. Wyon H.
Lt. Col.
Commanding 312 Brigade R.F.A.

Divl. Artillery

62nd Division.

312th BRIGADE, R. F. A.

J U L Y, 1 9 1 8.

Army Form C. 2118.

WAR DIARY of 312 Brigade M.T.A.
INTELLIGENCE SUMMARY.
No. 1 ORIGINAL
(Erase heading not required)

Instructions regarding War Diaries and Intelligence Summaries are contained in F. S. Regs., Part II. and the Staff Manual respectively. Title pages will be prepared in manuscript.

Place	Date	Hour	Summary of Events and Information	Remarks and references to Appendices
ORVILLE	July 1st to 14th		Brigade in rest and training at ORVILLE. (G.H.Q. & IV. Corps Reserve.)	App C
	15th	2.00 p.m.	Brigade entrained at DOULLENS (North & South) and MONDICOURT	App C / App L / App L
	16th	1.00 a.m.	Entrainment completed. Travelled via AMIENS and PARIS.	
Area of XXII Corps.	17th		Detrained. A Bty at MAILLY-le-CAMP. Halted for night at SOUDRON.	App L
			B " " " " "	
			C " ARCIS-LE "	
			D " SOMMESOUS " SOMMESOUS.	
	18th		Marched to ST MARD les ROUFFY (Ref. 50 Chalons 1/100,000 – French)	App L
	19th	6.30 a.m.	Marched to point 1 mile N. of AVENAY, where wagon lines were pitched in valley 1 km. E. of point 157. Col. EDEN, Bty Commanders and staffs met C.R.A. at GERMAINE and reconnoitred wood 2 roads in neighbourhood of Le Godat (CADRAN and MONTANEUF (Route for this days march FLAVIGNY, PLIVOT, OIRY, MAREUIL-sur-AY)	Ref. 50 CHALONS 1/100,000 & REIMS 1/100,000. App L
	20th	2.30 a.m.	Marched to position of readiness, head of column at cross roads immediately beneath N of Montaneuf on 34 REIMS. Waited there with Italian Artillery till 5.0 p.m	App C

WAR DIARY

of 312 Brigade M.R

INTELLIGENCE SUMMARY. Sheet No. 2.

Army Form C. 2118.

OM/C/MAZ

Place	Date	Hour	Summary of Events and Information	Remarks and references to Appendices
ECUEIL FARM	20th	5.0 p.m.	At 5.0 p.m. Brigade moved forward. A, B and D Bties went into action in woods W. of ECUEIL FARM: C B'y in copse 800 yards W. of COURTAGNON FARM: N.Q 750 yards S.E of ECUEIL FARM. During morning a shell fell in the waiting column and inflicted casualties:- N.Q. 1 killed B B'y 5 " : 8 wounded including 2/Lt. WHITWORTH and 2/Lt. BURT.	Ref. Map. F^ille de SONCHERY SUR-VESLE 1/20,000 JAC
"	21st	10.30 a.m. to 1.35 p.m.	Fired creeping barrage in support of attack by 187th Inf'y Bde and 9th D.L.I. This Brigade took left of zone from S. edge of BOIS de ROUVROY to N. end of BOIS des DIX HOMMÉES. Italian & French Artillery cooperated: 310 on night of 20/21. Fire ceased at 1.35: reported that all objectives were gained; this report was apparently erroneous. Weather intensely hot. During the action. 2 sergeants. 2 bombardiers and 1 gunner of D.B'y. were wounded by a shell.	JAC
"	22nd	12.15 p.m. to 2.15 p.m.	Fired creeping barrage on position of BOIS du PETIT CHAMP, N.W. of COITRON, in support of advance by 62nd Div'l Infantry. All objectives were reached, and prisoners and M.Gs. captured. 2/Lt. DRAPER & 2 men wounded at A B'y position	JAC
"	23rd	6.0 a.m. to 8.0 a.m.	Fired creeping barrage in support of attack by 62nd Div'l Infantry on MARFAUX and COITRON. The 120th Artillery, French. cooperated in this barrage with	JAC

Army Form C. 2118.

WAR DIARY
of 312 Brigade RFA
INTELLIGENCE SUMMARY.
(Erase heading not required.) Sheet No 3 original

Place	Date	Hour	Summary of Events and Information	Remarks and references to Appendices
ECUEIL FARM	23rd	11:00 a.m. to 1:0 p.m. 5:30 p.m. 7:30 p.m.	The artillery of this Divn; as did the XXII Corps Heavies & French Heavies. Operation successful. This Brigade assisted an attack by the French on left of 62nd Divn front by searching eastern slopes of the ARDRE VALLEY. By request of the French fired on BOIS des DIX HOMMÉES to support attack by French Colonial Divn. The attack was not successful, and fire was kept up on the wood at intervals during the night.	Ref. Map. Fille de JONCHERY SUR-VESLE
	24th		Weather turned wet in the early morning and there was much rain during the day. Fired bursts on BOIS des DIX HOMMÉES to help French Divn on our right. S.O.S. lines fixed 600 yards NW of MARFAUX. Harassed CHAUMUZY to SARCY ROAD. Enemy planes showed great daring flying low over battery positions.	
	25th 26th		" " artillery was more active, and this Bde had 11 casualties (10 w - 1 killed). Supported minor French operations in neighbourhood of BLIGNY. Enemy artillery fired many rounds, especially in neighbourhood of CBY. and around ECEUIL FARM. — Weather in afternoon turned very wet.	
	27th	6.0 a.m. to	Fired crashing barrage in support of attack by our divl infantry down ARDRE valley. F.O.O. reported that our infantry were advancing as fast as	

Army Form C. 2118.

WAR DIARY
of 312 Brigade R.F.A.
INTELLIGENCE SUMMARY. Sheet No. 4.   ORIGINAL

(Erase heading not required.)

Instructions regarding War Diaries and Intelligence Summaries are contained in F. S. Regs., Part II. and the Staff Manual respectively. Title pages will be prepared in manuscript.

Place	Date	Hour	Summary of Events and Information	Remarks and references to Appendices
	27- III	5.9 a.m.	our barrage permitted.	Ref. Map. JONCHERY SUR-VESLE 1/20,000.
		1.0 p.m.	Fired to support attack by 152 & 186 B.Inf". Bdes on CHAUMUZY. Barrage was lifted on to final line almost at once as infantry were meeting with little opposition. Batteries moved forward singly & before dark were all in position W. of POURCY. Weather — heavy rain. H.Q. moved to position vacated by C.B.Y.	
	28- III		Batteries moved forward at dawn to positions W. of MARFAUX. H.Q. in bank S.W. of MARFAUX. Supported advance of 185th Inf Bde on MONTAGNE DE BLIGNY, searched valley N. of Red line, & fired on reported enemy M.Gs. Weather improved.	
	29- III		S.O.S. lines laid down 300 yds. N. of RED LINE, N. of BLIGNY. Fired when called upon to deal with enemy machine guns. Front covered by this Div'l Artillery was shortened: 51st Div'l Arty took over on the left, French on the night. At 7.45 p.m. supported a clearing up operation by a company of 2/5 W. Yorks Reg⁺ on the MONTAGNE DE BLIGNY	
	30- III	5.0 a.m. 4.0 p.m. 11.0 a.m.	Batteries searched neighbourhood of SARCY. All batteries withdrew	

Army Form C. 2118.

WAR DIARY
312 Brigade RFA
INTELLIGENCE SUMMARY. Sheet No 5 ORIGINAL

(Erase heading not required.)

Place	Date	Hour	Summary of Events and Information	Remarks and references to Appendices
	30th	2.0 p.m.	Brigade rendezvous E of ST. IMOGES and marched via GERMAINE, AVENAY BISSEUIL, & TOURS-SUR-MARNE to AIGNY.	Ref: Map. 56 CHALONS/4 1/100,000
AIGNY.	31st		Rested at AIGNY	

Wilson Lt Col RFA
Commanding 312 Brigade RFA

Original

War Diary

of

312th Brigade, R.F.A.

Volume XX

From 1st August 1918
To 31st August 1918

ORIGINAL

Army Form C. 2118.

WAR DIARY of 312 Bde R.F.A.
INTELLIGENCE SUMMARY.
August 1918

Instructions regarding War Diaries and Intelligence Summaries are contained in F. S. Regs., Part II. and the Staff Manual respectively. Title pages will be prepared in manuscript.

(Erase heading not required.)

Place	Date	Hour	Summary of Events and Information	Remarks and references to Appendices
CHÂLONS-SUR-MARNE	August 1st		Brigade entrained at CHALONS and COOLUS and proceeded via CIRY-SUR-MARNE, PARIS, AMIENS to MONDICOURT	W.D/G.E.
BUS (LES ARTOIS)	2nd / 3rd	Night of 2nd/3rd	Brigade arrived at BUS. (LES ARTOIS)	W.D/G.E.
IV Corps	3rd to 14th		Remained at BUS in IV Corps Mobile Reserve. On the 13th "A B" was inspected by G.O.C. IV Corps vice G.O.C. 3rd Army.	W.D/G.E.
	15th		Wagon lines moved to HENU	W.D/G.E.
	16th		O.C. Brigade with B.C.'s reconnoitred for battery positions in F.20 (Ref.Map. 57 N.E. 1/20,000) Selected positions marked by F.S.Co.	W.D/G.E.
57 D.H.E. / 20,000	17th/18th	night	"D B" moved guns to positions, 3 left them there camouflaged but without personnel.	W.D/G.E.
ESSARTS	19th		"A B", "B" & "C B" moved guns to selected positions, 3 left them there N.O. moved to trench E. of HENNESCAMP. Lt. Col. EDEN took command of group, 310 and 312 Bdes. "B B" brought up guns.	W.D/G.E.
	20th			W.D/G.E.
	21st	4.55am / 7.37a.m.	Fired barrage in support of 37th Division who attacked S. of ABLAINZEVILLE to depth of 2500 yds. Operation successful. B"s remained in F.20.	W.D/G.E.

ORIGINAL

2.

Army Form C. 2118.

WAR DIARY of 312 Bde R.F.A.
or
INTELLIGENCE SUMMARY. August 1918

(Erase heading not required.)

Place	Date	Hour	Summary of Events and Information	Remarks and references to Appendices
PUISIEUX ESSARTS	22nd		B'ty remained in F.26 till night, when they moved forward to positions chosen in L.15, N.E. of PUISIEUX. Lt Col. SHERLOCK D.S.O. took over command of Group.	D.11/9/e
PUISIEUX AU-MONT 57 D NE	23rd	11:00 a.m. 12 midday 3:30 to 4:10 pm	Fixed barrage in support of attack by 5th Division S.E. of MIRAUMONT. Infantry advanced successfully; were counter-attacked and Brigade fired barrage S.O.S. in their support. R.E. Seton at B'de H.Q. had one man wounded, no casualties in batteries	D.11/9/e
			During afternoon barrage orders were received to move to CONTAY. Later orders substituted BERTRANCOURT as destination. Batteries marched to various with Wagon lines at BERTRANCOURT, arriving too late to comply with orders to be in action at 1.5 a.m. near ENGELBELMER ville.	D.11/9/e
BERTRANCOURT		8:0 am [?] midnight		
Area of V Corps	24th		Marched at 8.0 a.m. to rendez-vous in P.23d, where C.Os 310 & 312 Bdes F.B.Cs had a conference with C.R.A. 38th Division. B.Cs reconnoitred positions on Eastern bank of river ANCRE, which had been won during the night. Batteries moved by temporary bridge at AVELUY and occupied positions in W.11 b & d (57 D.S.E. 1/20,000.) H.Q. in N.W. of MARTINSART.	D.11/9/e
POZIERES	25th		The enemy were reported to have retired out of range; batteries forward to R.33d, S.H.Q. to same neighbourhood in daylight	D.11/9/e

ORIGINAL

Army Form C. 2118.

WAR DIARY of 312 Bde R.F.A.

INTELLIGENCE SUMMARY

AUGUST 1918

Instructions regarding War Diaries and Intelligence Summaries are contained in F.S. Regs., Part II. and the Staff Manual respectively. Title pages will be prepared in manuscript.

(Erase heading not required.)

Place	Date	Hour	Summary of Events and Information	Remarks and references to Appendices
FEZIERES	26	3.20 a.m. / 2.40 p.m.	B/ty fired destructive and harassing fire on BAZENTIN-LE-PETIT and LONGUEVAL in preparation for an attack by 114th Div. 38th Division. Capture of HIGH WOOD and BAZENTIN was unhauled at midday. H.Q. moved during afternoon to position near MARTINPUICH and BAZENTIN.	
57 D.S.C. 1/20,000				
HIGH WOOD				
57 S.W. 1/20,000	27	4.30 a.m. / 7.30 a.m.	t. S.11.b. This Brigade was allotted to 115th Inf. Bde for co-operation. Fired barrage to assist advance by 114th Bde towards FLERS and LONGUEVAL. Harassing fire at intervals on reported points. Situation was obscure during day. A/By moved forward during day to E. of BAZENTIN & D/By to t S10c. H.Q. to S8c.	
	28		B/By moved to S15a. Harassing fire but down on lanes allotted in front of FLERS to LONGUEVAL Road, no advance being made by infantry.	
	29	5.15 a.m / 7.00 a.m.	B/By fired barrage in support of advance towards MORVAL. Enemy had withdrawn in the night and advance was unopposed. FLERS and DELVILLE WOOD were occupied and line advanced E. of midge in T8 and T9 still held by enemy M.G.s. B/ty moved up to T7 before midday and engaged in harassing fire. N.Q. S12 b. 28.	
LONGUEVAL FLERS	30		A. & B. B/ty moved 1500 yards east in order to bring SAILLY-SAILLISEL within range. Harassed N2b and eastwards. Enemy artillery active.	
	31		Same positions. Enemy artillery afterwards unable to shell W. of T9 central.	

Casualties during month. 26th B.B.y. 2 killed, 1 missing, 2 wounded
27th " D " 2 wounded.

Secret

9821

312 Brigade RFA

WAR DIARY

ORIGINAL

Volume IX

From 1st September 1918
to 30th September 1918

Army Form C. 2118.

ORIGINAL

WAR DIARY /312 Bde R.F.A.
INTELLIGENCE SUMMARY
Month of Sept. 1918.

(Erase heading not required.)

Place	Date	Hour	Summary of Events and Information	Remarks and references to Appendices
DELVILLE WOOD. III Army IV Corps 38th Div.	Sept. 1st		Brigade remained in action in T7 & T8 (57°S.W.) Probably move forward countermanded on report of continued resistance at MORVAL.	W/W.C.
	2nd		Moved forward E of MORVAL, and occupied positions N. of COMBLES (H.Q. HAIE WOOD. A/312, B/312 and C/312 in T7: D/312 in U13.	W/W.C. W/W.C.E.
COMBLES		5.0 p.m. 7.40 p.m.	Fixed barrage in support of advance by 115th Infy Bde from SAILLY-SAILLISEL towards MESNIL-EN-ARROUAISE. No advance was made, and at midnight enemy were reported to be still in SAILLY and counter-attacking. D/312 retired to T17.	W/W.C.E. W/W.C.E.
	3rd		Positions unchanged. Infy patrols were reported to be feeling way towards MESNIL and meeting little opposition.	W/W.C.E.
			H.Q. moved to sunken road S. of MESNIL (U5c 1-2). D/312 came into action in same road: B/312 1000 yards W. of village. A/312 and C/312 remained in yesterday's positions in readiness. Orders were sent them to move up to U11d: while they were moving enemy counter attacked our infantry who had worked the CANAL DU NORD at MANANCOURT. A/312 & C/312 fell into action beside B/312 and fired on trenches in V21 (57°S.E) in which the enemy were clearly seen to be massing. Enemy counter attack was repulsed. — At night four large fires were burning in enemy lines.	W/W.C.E. W/W.C.E.
MESNIL-EN- ARROUAISE.	4th			

ORIGINAL

Army Form C. 2118.

WAR DIARY / 312 Bde R.F.A.
or
INTELLIGENCE SUMMARY. Sept 1918.

(Erase heading not required.)

Instructions regarding War Diaries and Intelligence
Summaries are contained in F. S. Regs., Part II.
and the Staff Manual respectively. Title pages
will be prepared in manuscript.

ORIGINAL

Place	Date	Hour	Summary of Events and Information	Remarks and references to Appendices
MESNIL ETRICOURT att 21st Divn	Sept 5	5.0 a.m.	38th Divn was relieved by 21st Divn during night 4th – 5th. Bombarded trenches V28 & V16. Progress was made on both flanks. B/312 & C/312 moved forward to positions in U.14. A/312 & D/312 remained in yesterdays positions. During harassing fire one Hay of D/312 blew up killing Sgt Weaver & 2/OR & wounding 7 OR. H.Q. moved to canal bank in ETRICOURT. B/312 & D/312 crossed canal to positions in V.14. All batteries were out of range by midday.	W.J.G.E. W.J.G.E.
	6th			W.J.G.E.
	7th		This Bde was relieved by 315th Army Brigade. Bus drew out to W.L. near COMBLES.	W.J.G.E.
COURCELLES VIEUX Corps BEUGNY VI Corps 62nd Divn HAVRINCOURT	8th 9th 10th 11th 12th 13th	5.25 a.m 4.50 am	Marched north. Head of Bde. left LES BOEUFS at 8.0 a.m. Went via TILLOY, GREVILLERS to COURCELLES (VI Corps Area) to rejoin 62nd Divn & to meet (J36 (57c N.E. 1/20,000). C.O. & B.Cs reconnoitred positions in J36. Bde moved at midday to BEUGNY. Bde occupied positions in J36. H.Q. in same dug out as that occupied 19-11-17. Fired barrage in support of attack by our army on HAVRINCOURT. Village captured but not final objective. Bn fired on many MG calls and on points reported to be held by enemy. Enemy counter attacked & infantry gave ground to E of HAVRINCOURT village.	W.J.G.E. W.J.G.E. W.J.G.E. W.J.G.E. W.J.G.E.

ORIGINAL

Army Form C. 2118.

WAR DIARY / 312 Bde. R.F.A.
or
INTELLIGENCE SUMMARY. Sept: 1918.
(Erase heading not required.)

OP4/G/1942

Instructions regarding War Diaries and Intelligence Summaries are contained in F. S. Regs., Part II. and the Staff Manual respectively. Title pages will be prepared in manuscript.

Place	Date	Hour	Summary of Events and Information	Remarks and references to Appendices
HAVRINCOURT VI Corps 62nd Div.	Sept 14th	5.20 6.17	Fixed barrage to secure KIMBER TRENCH, final objective of operation of 12th inst. Operation successful.	6/WE
	15th		Fewer counter-preparation before dawn day. Counter-preparation returned. Less artillery. By 3rd Bde Bowling/plans army 62nd Divn active at night, our large/plane brought it down at W.L. Lt WILLIAMS M.C. wounded.	6/WE
	16th		Fixed counter-preparation at dawn.	6/WE
	17th		A quiet day. Some increase in enemy artillery fire.	6/WE
	18th	7.25am 3.30pm 5.0pm	To assist IV Corps in minor operation fired a smoke barrage S. of FLESQUIÈRES. An intense barrage was put down on whole area occupied by the Bde. at 3.30 p.m. Major ARNAUD FOSTER reported from his O.P that an attack against the Divisional front. S.O.S. was sent to all batteries at 3.35 pm. By 3.40 pm all communication went out. The barrage was of exceptional intensity, all calibres and shells. Orders were carried by runners, and all batteries continued to fire till 5.20 - 5.30 p.m., when the order to cease fire was received from our artillery fire - S.O.S. & counter was made on the divisional front at 5.0 pm and caused many casualties among the enemy. Preparation was reported to have caused the enemy. The attack was repulsed. Total casualties in Bde. 1 killed Officer (2nd Lt TUSSIK. B/312) 2 O.R's wounded.	6/WE

ORIGINAL

Army Form C. 2118.

WAR DIARY /312 Bde R.F.A. Sept. 1918.
or
INTELLIGENCE SUMMARY.
(Erase heading not required.)

Place	Date	Hour	Summary of Events and Information	Remarks and references to Appendices
HAURINCOURT VII Corps 3rd Div.	Sept 19.		Position unchanged. Div'l line completely restored as before yesterdays attack.	E.J.G.E.
	20.		Wire cutting commenced in R.29 by D/312.	E.J.G.E.
	21.			
	22.	3:45 p.m. 4:30 p.m.	Helped an operation by 63rd Div on night by firing on R.24a. Considerable movement of enemy infantry was observed and fired on. Enemy movement still noticeable. Centres of movement were heavily crashed and harassed both by day & night. Our area heavily bombed at night. Enemy artillery more active and HF calls showed that he had batteries in action within 3000 yards of his front line. Movement of infantry much diminished.	E.J.G.E. E.J.G.E. E.J.G.E.
	23.		Col Eden went on leave: Major Arnold Forster D.S.O. took command of Bde. Enemy artillery very quiet. No movement visible in his lines. Ditto.	E.J.G.E. E.J.G.E.
	24. 25. 26. 27.	5:20 a.m. 10:50 a.m.	Enemy artillery distinctly more active, especially with long range H.V. guns. Bde fired barrage in support of 9th Infy Brigade in their advance on RIBECOURT, part of general advance by 1st 3rd Armies to cross the CANAL DE L'ESCAUT. First 3 second objectives were captured according to programme Z Brigade was ordered to move forward at 10:50 a.m. Positions were selected and occupied in R.34, whence number forward in L.31.b.3d, repaired to be still held by enemy was fired on. F.O.Os went forward by K.36 & reported targets, and that our troops were working forward towards MARCOING. Hostile batteries in K.15 were engaged	E.J.G.E. E.J.G.E. E.J.G.E.

ORIGINAL

Army Form C. 2118.

Instructions regarding War Diaries and Intelligence
Summaries are contained in F. S. Regs., Part II.
and the Staff Manual respectively. Title pages
will be prepared in manuscript.

WAR DIARY /312 Bde R.F.A.
or
INTELLIGENCE SUMMARY.
Sept. 1918.
(Erase heading not required.)

ORIGINAL

Place	Date	Hour	Summary of Events and Information	Remarks and references to Appendices
RIBECOURT	Sept. 28.	4.30 a.m. 5.50 a.m.	Fixed barrage to cover advance E. of RIBECOURT by 187th Bde.	W/GE
		6.45 a.m. 7.10 a.m.	Fixed barrage to cover renewed advance of 187th Bde on MARCOING. The Infantry advances were successful, and in the afternoon batteries moved up to L26. E. of RIBECOURT. H.Q. to L31.b.	W/GE W/GE
	29.	7.30 a.m 9.10 a.m	To support advance on MASHIERES by 187th Bde in conjunction with 2nd Div 3 N.Z. Dio. This Bde fired a barrage. MASNIERES was captured but as the enemy still held commanding ground E. of Canal, it was impossible to bring the batteries forward. Fire on trenches held by the enemy in G.29.3, G.29(57)B.N.W.) Bde moved forward to L28 (N.Q. L34 b.1.6.) and prepared to fire barrage to support attack on RUMILLY on following morning.	W/GE W/GE
MARCOING	30.			

F. A. Arnold-Forster
Major
O.C. 312 Brigade R.F.A.

SECRET

WAR DIARY

312 BRIGADE

R.F.A

ORIGINAL

Volume XXII

From 1st October 1918
To 31st October 1918

Army Form C. 2118.

ORIGINAL

WAR DIARY 312 BRIGADE R.F.A.
INTELLIGENCE SUMMARY. OCTOBER 1918.

(Erase heading not required.)

Place	Date October	Hours	Summary of Events and Information	Remarks and references to Appendices
MARCOING. VI Corps. 62nd D.A. (SHERLOCK GROUP)	1st	0430 to 0700.	H.Q. at L.34.b. Batteries in L.28.b. (Ref. Map 57C N.E 1/20,000) Fixed Barrage on RUMILLY in support of advance by 62nd Division. Stiff resistance was met with, and enemy counter attacked.	W.M.G.E. W.M.G.E.
		1802 to 1915.	Fixed Barrage to support renewed attempt to secure the morning's objective. RUMILLY and trench to east of village were made good. During the day three 77 mm. guns abandoned by the enemy W. of the canal were brought into action, and used for harrassing fire. Enemy artillery fire considerable E. of Canal. One 77 mm. gun shell burst in this Bde H.Q. killing Sgt. Artificer GALE and slight to W. One 77 mm. gun shell burst in this Bde H.Q. killing Sgt. Artificer GALE and seriously wounding three men. Casualties in B'ies I O.R.	W.M.G.E. W.M.G.E. W.M.G.E.
	2nd		Positions unchanged. O.P.s established in RUMILLY, and batteries engaged in harrassing fire and fire on observed targets. 3rd Division took over front of 62nd Division. Positions unchanged.	W.M.G.E.
3rd D.A. (SHERLOCK GROUP)	3rd 4th 5th		" "	
MARCOING. 3rd D.A. (MAIR GROUP)	6th		Brigade crossed the CANAL DE L'ESCAUT at MARCOING, relieving the 34th A.F.A. H.Q. in dug-out on railway L.18.b (57C N.E); batteries in G.13.d (57B N.W.). All batteries were in action by midday and registered during afternoon. On this day, and the following morning 1000 rounds H.E. and Gas were fired from two 105 mm. Hows. abandoned by the enemy on the positions now occupied by us.	W.M.G.E.

Army Form C. 2118.

ORIGINAL

WAR DIARY 312 BDE R.F.A.
INTELLIGENCE SUMMARY OCTOBER 1918.

(Erase heading not required.)

Place	Date	Hour	Summary of Events and Information	Remarks and references to Appendices
MARCOING. VI Corps. 3rd D.A.	October 7th		Positions unchanged. Enemy continued to shell W.L.W. of MARCOING, as they had during the last week, causing four casualties among the gunners, and killing many horses. W/E	
	8th	04.30 to 07.32	Brigade fired barrage from G.23 (57B.N.W.) to N.E. of SERANVILLERS, covering advance of 9th Infy Bde, 3rd Division. The objective was secured, but the enemy was reported to be holding FORENVILLE and road S. of this hamlet with M.Gs. W/E	
		12.35 to 13.00	Fired barrage on road mentioned above (N8c 6.2 - H14b 4.2), which on our subsequent advance was found littered with dead and wounded Germans. W/E	
RUMILLY.			Bde moved up in the evening to positions in the open 1500 yards E. of ROMILLY (G.17, 22, 23.) The enemy counterattacked fiercely at NIERGNIES and harrassed the whole area of our advance with his artillery. In spite of this the batteries were in action by nightfall with only four casualties. Communication was maintained with H.Q. by an intermediate station at G.21 central. W/E	
Guards D.A.			Command of the Brigade passed to Guards Divn at midnight. Weather bright and cool. W/W/E	
SERANVILLERS.	9th	05.20 to 06.45	Fired barrage from E. edge of WAMBAIX to railway in H.11. Enemy were found to have retreated out of touch, and to be shelling villages considerably to the East of us. Brigade was ordered to advance to positions of observation at SERANVILLERS. Batteries were in action in H.19.b by midday. H.Q. at CHATEAU FARM in the village. After 13.00 hours the enemy shelled battery area with a light N.V. gun, and caused five casualties to G.R.a. W/W/E	

Army Form C. 2118.

WAR DIARY 312 Bde R.F.A.
or
INTELLIGENCE SUMMARY. OCTOBER 1917.

ORIGINAL

Place	Date	Hours	Summary of Events and Information	Remarks and references to Appendices
CATTENIÈRES. ESTOURMEL. Guards D.A.	October 10.	1030.	Bde took up positions of readiness in Hill. H.Q. in ESTOURMEL. Brigade went into Divisional Reserve and settled down to await further orders in the positions now occupied.	W.T.E
62nd D.A.	11 to 13.	0500.	Command of Brigade handed back to 62nd D.A. Positions unchanged.	W.T.E
	14.		Lt Col: R.H. JOHNSON D.S.O. took command of the Brigade, and was subsequently posted as from this date.	W.T.E
	15.		Positions unchanged.	W.T.E
QUIÉVY Guards D.A. 62nd D.A.	16.		Brigade moved forward. H.Q. to QUIÉVY, Batteries to positions in D9310.(57 BN.E.) 2500 yards W. of SOLESMES. S.O.S. lines were laid out to E. of SOLESMES. Brigade was under command of Guards D.A. for this night, reverting to 62nd D.A. in the morning. Weather broke: heavy rain.	W.T.E
	17 to 19.		For forthcoming operations this Brigade and 310 Bde were organised as JOHNSON GROUP in liaison with 186 Infy Brigade. For these three days the batteries lay in the open, their position being in a fold off the ground behind a crest in full view of the enemy. Hostile harassing fire was at times heavy, but only four casualties were incurred. Weather continued very wet. From crest in front there was excellent observation of the enemy's position.	W.T.E
	20	0200 to 0420	As part of an operation by the 3rd Army, having for object the carrying of the line of the SELLE RIVER, this Bde fired a creeping barrage in support of advance by	

Army Form C. 2118.

WAR DIARY, 312 BDE R.F.A.
INTELLIGENCE SUMMARY. OCTOBER 1918.

(Erase heading not required.)

Place	Date	Hour	Summary of Events and Information	Remarks and references to Appendices
QUIEVY - SOLESMES 62nd D.A.	20	0200 to 0420	186th Infy Bde from E. edge of SOLESMES to E. of high ground by PIGEON BLANC (S7 B N.E. and S1 A S.E.) Advance went according to programme, and at 0950 O.P. was established at PIGEON BLANC. W/Q2	Appendix A. Congratulatory message from G.O.C. 186 Infy Bde on this day's barrage.
		0745 to 0925	Fired further barrage in support of advance by 185 Infy Bde towards ROMERIES. W/Q2	
		1400 to 1430	On report of hostile counter-attack on night of our front, fired at slow rate on final protective barrage. Cease Fire ordered on report of slackening of enemy effort. W/Q2	
		1600 to 1630	Fired to keep down M.G. activity in orchards W. of river at ROMERIES. W/Q2	
ST PYTHON	21.		Batteries moved forward at half-hour intervals from 0900 hours, crossed the river SELLE at ST PYTHON and occupied positions on E. edge of that village. In the afternoon heavy fire was put down around the battery positions, and seven casualties inflicted. H.Q. to curé's house in ST PYTHON. W/Q2	
SOLESMES	22.		At 1700 hours H.Q. were moved to SOLESMES to be ready for operations on the 23rd. Battery positions unchanged. Enemy continued to shell ST PYTHON and SOLESMES. LT. CRANE, 9th D.L.I. attd for observation duty to this Bde) was wounded. W/Q2	
3rd D.A.	23.	0420 to 0630	As part of continued advance by 3rd Army this Bde fired a barrage to cover advance of 8th Infy Bde, through VERTAIN. This advance being successful	
		0840 to 10.20	this Bde fired to cover further advance on ESCARMAIN. W/Q2 At midday, 8th Infy Bde decided to move forward to VERTAIN. This Brigade	

Army Form C. 2118.

ORIGINAL

WAR DIARY, 312 Bde R.F.A.
INTELLIGENCE SUMMARY OCTOBER 1918.

(Erase heading not required.)

Instructions regarding War Diaries and Intelligence Summaries are contained in F. S. Regs., Part II. and the Staff Manual respectively. Title pages will be prepared in manuscript.

Place	Date	Hour	Summary of Events and Information	Remarks and references to Appendices
VERTAIN. 3rd D.A.	23rd		accompanied them and by 1715 two batteries were in action E. of VERTAIN: the other two batteries were in by 1930. H.Q. in the village. W.H.E.	
	24th	0420 to 0752.	Fired barrage from PONT DE BUAT to N.E. of RUESNES (51.A.S.E) in support of advance by 9th Inf.y Brigade. This advance was successful and at 0800 b.m. an immediate move forward to about W 6 a was ordered. Positions were reconnoitred and occupied. There (E. of ESCARMAIN). Battery W.L. which had been at St PYTHON since the 21st were brought forward to ESCARMAIN. The position of the enemy was obscure and no firing was done from these positions. W.H.E.	
ESCARMAIN.	25th		Positions unchanged. W.H.E.	
62nd D.A.	26th		Whole Brigade moved to Corps Reserve at QUIÉVY. W.H.E.	
	27th to 31st.		Remained in rest at QUIÉVY. W.H.E.	

W Johnson Lt Col. R.F.A.

1/11/18.

APPENDIX A.

Army Form C. 2118.

WAR DIARY, 312 BDE R.F.A.
INTELLIGENCE SUMMARY. OCTOBER 1918.
(Erase heading not required.)

Extract from letter from Brigadier General J.C.BURNETT D.S.O
G.O.C. 186th Infantry Brigade 62nd.Division to Brigadier General
A.T.Anderson C.M.G., Commanding 62nd. Divisional Artillery.

"Both the Left attacking Battalions and the one which took the
"Railway Station at SOLESMES wish me to say that it was the most
"accurate barrage which they have advanced under.
"Would you please convey my thanks to the men behind the guns who
"so largely contributed towards the success"

                    (sd) J.G.BURNETT
                            Brigadier General

23.10.1918

Army Form C. 2118.

WAR DIARY
or
INTELLIGENCE SUMMARY.
(Erase heading not required.)

WAR DIARY.
312th Brigade. R.F.A.

NOVEMBER

ORIGINAL

Volume XVIII

SHEET 1.   ORIGINAL.

Army Form C. 2118.

WAR DIARY
or
INTELLIGENCE SUMMARY.
(Erase heading not required.)

3/2 H. Bde. R.F.A.

Place	Date	Hours	Summary of Events and Information	Remarks and references to Appendices
QUIÉVY.	1.11.18	0900.	Orders received from Div. Arty. that Bde. Commanders were to report at D.A. SOLESMES at 1100 hours. Receiving orders, positions were reconnoitred in neighbourhood north of RUESNES. Following positions taken A/312 R.B.C.A.1. B/312 R.B.C.1.8. C/312.R.B.C.1.0. D/312 R.B.d.O.O. 400 rounds per gun were ordered up. The first had going up at dusk	51.A. 1/40. " " 51.A. " " " " " " " " " JMcS
		1630.	The order that batteries would take up positions on night of 2/3 was altered to 3/4, to allow of all available teams being used for ammunition	JMcS
QUIÉVY.	2.11.18	1230.	Batteries moved to the VERTAIN-ESCARMAIN area starting at 1230 hours. HQ/312. A/312. C/312 unmained at VERTAIN B/312. D/312 went to ESCARMAIN, both villages being full to overflowing. During night a concentration by H.V. guns was put down on B/312 who lost 48 horses, 24 being killed. The Bomb. and two men on piquet duty being wounded	57.A. 1/40. 51.A. " " " " JMcS
GEELVERTAIN	3.11.18		"JOHNSON" GROUP to be formed of 310, 312 Bdes. R.F.A under command of	JMcS

SHEET 2 ORIGINAL

Army Form C. 2118.

WAR DIARY
or
INTELLIGENCE SUMMARY.
(Erase heading not required.)

312th Bde. RFA

Place	Date	Hours	Summary of Events and Information	Remarks and references to Appendices
RUESNES.	3/11/18		Lieut. Col. Johnson. D.S.O. accordingly during morning GROUP H.Q. were established with 186, 187 Inf: Bdes. at Farm R.20.b.3.7. just south of	51.A. 1/40
		1300.	RUESNES. Communications were established running round rear of village, these only cut once some 3 hours after the battle started. Batteries moved up into positions at 2100 hours nearing HA BEAUDIGNIES	" " " 57.A. "
		2130.	and RUESNES. All batteries reported in action by 2130 hours. No hostile artillery activity reported. No battery was up to midnight.	" " JKJ
RUESNES	4/11/18	0530.	Zero Hour. A creeping barrage started on the whole Corps Front on the right by 3rd, 62nd Div: Arty., + 76. A.F.A.B., covering the 62 Div on the left by A. Arty. covering the Guards. Started on general line R.3.d.5.4.— R.7.c.5.6. and advanced to line R.6.d.2.8.— M.7.d.9.5.— R.18.c.5.3. reaching this line by 3hr+97. And resting here some 300x in front of the BLUE LINE until the guards on the left pushed into line. At 3hr + 144 the barrage was continued running due East finishing on line M.4.d.4.2.— Cluster of FRASNOY — M.16.c.0.1. resting here as a	51.A. 1/40 " " " 51.A. 51.1/40 " " " " " " " " " " " " 51. 1/40 JKJ

SHEET 3.   ORIGINAL

Army Form C. 2118.

WAR DIARY
or
INTELLIGENCE SUMMARY.
(Erase heading not required.)

3/2ⁿᵈ Bde. R.F.A

Place	Date	Hours	Summary of Events and Information	Remarks and references to Appendices
RUESNES	4.11.18	0650	Protective barrage for 10 minutes. At 0850 76 A.F.A.Bde. were reported in action in R.10.b. By 0945 guards were reported on feen line.	51 1/40
		0945	(FRASNOY - VILLEREAU) Batteries start to move forward B/312 leading	"
		1045	HQ BELLEVUE FARM (R.15.b.7.7.) and bridge in R.11.C.41. Batteries pushed straight forward took up positions in neighbourhood of L'ORGNIES, M.G. fire being met with by reconnoitring parties in direction of LE QUESNOY. Positions taken up as follows :- H.Q./312 R.12.a.3.2. A/312. M.15.C.3.6. B/312. M.14.C.5.3. C/312. M.13.a.0.2. D/312. M.14.a.4.0. 310 Bde. being still in 'JOHNSON' Group had H.Q. at R.12.b.8.3. with position in M.14.15. and R.18.C. The 185 Inf. Bde. with whom this cooperating kept to shooting	51. 1/40. " " " " " " " "
LA BELLE MAISON			Hrs. at BELLE THE MAKE LA BELLE MAISON. (M.B.C.) C/312 fired a few rounds of harassing fire otherwise no fire from Bde. during evening. In bring up teams through RUESNES D/312 lost their B.S.M. killed and Lieut. Birch wounded.	51. 1/40. " J.N.G.

SHEET 4.

ORIGINAL

Army Form C. 2118.

312th Bde. R.F.A.

WAR DIARY
or
INTELLIGENCE SUMMARY.
(Erase heading not required.)

Place	Date	Hours	Summary of Events and Information	Remarks and references to Appendices
R.12.c.8.3	5.11.18	0600	Orders came through last night that 165 Inf. Bde. would attack at 0600 hours this morning. Consequently the Bde. put down a creeping barrage starting on gun-of line PETIT MARAIS (M.11.c.) — M.14.e. — TOUS VENTS (M.18.c.) — and finished with a 10 minute protective barrage on the line N.7.c.5.1. — SAHLOTON (N.14.d.9.0) at 30 + 60 – 70. The attack proved a complete success, little opposition being met with. By 0730 hours batteries were ready to move but were awaiting further orders.	51.A. 1/40.
L'ORGNIES AREA		0700		57. 1/40
		0730		" "
				" "
GOMMEGNIES		0630	Bde. H.Q. closed at R.12.a.3.2. and moved forward GOMMEGNIES (N.7.c.7.0.) Batteries remaining in the L'ORGNIES area, where they were billetted for the night. Communications by mounted orderly.	51 1/40 57.A " MN2
GOMMEGNIES LE CATEE. N.7.c.6.2.	6.11.18	0900 to 1130	During morning batteries moved up from L'ORGNIES area to the area around LE GRAND SART. (N.14.a) Mà FRASNOY (M.10.) and GOMMEGNIES. (N.7.c.) All batteries found billets for men, horses being chiefly in the open. Enemy hostile artillery activity with 10.5 cm. howrs. on chief crossing M.12.d.4.3. X Roads N.8.c. and CHEVAL BLANC (N.14.6)	51.A 1/40 57 1/40 " " " " MN2 "

SHEET 5 ORIGINAL

Army Form C. 2118.

WAR DIARY
INTELLIGENCE SUMMARY.

of 312th Bde. R.F.A.

Place	Date	Hours	Summary of Events and Information	Remarks and references to Appendices
LE CAYEE N.7.c.6.3.	7/11/18.		The 188 Inf. Bde. attacked from the general line of the BAVAI-PONT-SUR-SAMBRE (I.19.20 - O.11.) Supported by the 310 Bde. R.F.A. no longer under JOHNSON Group. 312. Bde. horsed forward from the LE SART-GOMMEGNIES area MA MORMAL FOREST (N.22.23.24.), OBI65(N.12.d.) O.7.a. - LE TIMON	51. 1/40. " " " " "
		1200	(O.8.d.) Billetting parties arriving about 1200 hours here subjected to active hostile harassing fire by 10.5 cm hows. Batteries arrived	
		1600.	by 1600 hours good billets having been found for all men in LE TIMON. H.Q. here at LE PONT DE POULE (O.8.d. 5.4) owing to its proximity with the 185 187 Inf Bde (O.8.d. O.8.)	57. 1/40 JMS "
LE TIMON	8/11/18.	O200	Orders received at O200 hours that 187 Inf. Bde: would advance from the general line HARGNIES (Q.24) - LA LONGUÉVAL (I.36.) to AVESNES - MAUBERGE - MONS road with support of 42nd & 310th Bdes. R.F.A. The 312th Bde. to take over from 310 at the elevation of the passage. Accordingly batteries here reconnoitred just west of NEUF MESNIL (P.16.) and Batteries moved forward MA GOGNIAUX - QUÉNE AU LOUP - COUTANT - (O.9.d.) (O.8.f.) (O.16.f.)	57. 1/40. " " " " JMS

SHEET 6   ORIGINAL

Army Form C. 2118.

372nd Bde, R.F.A.

WAR DIARY
or
INTELLIGENCE SUMMARY.

Place	Date	Hours	Summary of Events and Information	Remarks and references to Appendices
LE TIMON	6.11.18	1030	Pulling into positions of readiness on the COUTANT (0.16.6.) - L'ERMITAGE (O.11.C) road. Orders given to B/3/2. D/3/2. to go forward into positions	51. 1/40
		1120.	of observation in P.13.6. and P.14.d. Orders given to A/3/12 C/3/12 who had previously advanced to P.15.6. for reading positions to go into	" "
		1330.	positions of observation in P.14.d. P.13.6. Batteries in position A/3/12 P.14.d.9.5. B/3/12 P.14.C.2.7. C/3/12 P.13.6.6.1. D/3/12 P.15.6.5.1. reporting	" "
		1345.	in action via Telephone communication by 1345 hours. Batteries fired	" "
		1430.	Short barrage in support of 5th K.O.Y.L.I.s who were attempting to take FORT GRÉYAUX (P.11.d) the exploit failing. A/3/12 lost Their 2 being killed, 33 horses 16 being killed in getting into action between X Roads P.20.a. and their position P.14.d.9.5. No night firing	JM "
P.14.C.2.6.			HQ now with B/3/12 at P.14.C.2.6.	
P.14.C.2.6. TRI-MOUTON AREA.	9/11/18.		Orders came through late last night that 5th K.O.Y.L.I.s would try to capture FORT GRÉYAUX at whose disposal D/3/2 was placed. The 2/4th K.O.Y.L.I.s would cross ridge at P.23.C. and take high ground South	51. 1/40. " " " UK2"

SHEET 7.   ORIGINAL.

Army Form C. 2118.

312th Bde. R.F.A.

WAR DIARY
INTELLIGENCE SUMMARY
(Erase heading not required.)

Place	Date	Hours	Summary of Events and Information	Remarks and references to Appendices
P.14.c.2.6. TRINNCTON AREA.	9.11.18.	0500	of river B/312 being at Neu Chabonal. Full arrangements between O.E. D/312 & O.E. B/312 and O.C.S Inf. Btns. Enemy retired during night. Patrols reported FORT GRÉYAUX clear of the Enemy. No infantry fighting took place SOUS-LE-BOIS (Q.7.) and MAUBERGE (Q.3.) being taken without opposition. A line being established on the line ELESMES — ASSEVANT. During morning batteries moved up into positions of readiness observations in area Q.7. P.12. craters at P.15.b.7.2. and P.16.b.o.6. delaying advance until roads round were constructed. Positions were taken up as follows A/3/2 Q.1.c.8.3. B/3/2. C/312. P.6.c.3.8. D/312. Q.7.b.3.6. 'as two were established on a line 300' East of line of river Q.7.e. Though Inf. patrols were reported in BOUSSOIS (L.33.a.) H.Q. in SOUS-LE-BOIS Q.8.c.0.4.	51. 1/40 " " " " " " " " " " " JNP
SOUS-LE-BOIS. Q.7.	10.11.18.	1000	Batteries remain in action though Cavalry & Infantry patrols reported by contact plane in neighbourhood of BOUSSOIS (L.33.a.). All bridges (other HAUTMONT (P.23) and MAUBERGE (Q.3.) reported blown down. Pontoon bridge constructed at Q.14.a.3.7. 186 Inf. Bde take over front from 187 Bde.	51. 1/40 " " " JNP

SHEET. B.   ORIGINAL.

Army Form C. 2118.

372ⁿᵈ Bde. R.F.A.

WAR DIARY
or
INTELLIGENCE SUMMARY

(Erase heading not required.)

Place	Date	Hour	Summary of Events and Information	Remarks and references to Appendices
SOUS-LE-BOIS Q.7.	11.11.18	0600.	Report received that GERMANY had signed the Armistice and hostilities	51/ 1/40. JKP.
		1100.	ceased at 1100 hours. All guns were left in Sous. Bois.	
SOUS-LE-BOIS Q.7.	12.11.18		Terms of Armistice received, report including information that 62ⁿᵈ Div. would be one of those divisions to march into GERMANY. Accordingly general cleaning up was begun amongst batteries at once. The march to commence in all probability on the 17th. Lecture in "working in trails" by Division commander on overhauling etc. Brig. Gen. Andrews visited batteries informally to see how general cleaning up was progressing.	51/ 1/40. " " " " " JKP.
SOUS-LE-BOIS Q.7.	13.11.18			51/ 1/40. JKP.
SOUS-LE-BOIS Q.7.	14.11.18		Medical Inspection of all Batteries and H.Q. for purpose of weeding out the march into GERMANY. Orders received that all batteries were to be reduced to four gun batteries. Bde. H.Q. to remain unchanged	51/ 1/40. " " JKP.

SHEET. 9. ORIGINAL.

Army Form C. 2118.

3/2 K Bde. R.F.A

WAR DIARY
or
INTELLIGENCE SUMMARY.
(Erase heading not required.)

Place	Date	Hour	Summary of Events and Information	Remarks and references to Appendices
SOUS-LE BOIS Q.7.	15.11.18		Spent in reorganizing the batteries into a four gun battery basis; casting off the worst horses and reforming teams.	51. 1/40. "WD"
SOUS LE BOIS Q.7.	16.11.18		Surplus guns, wagons, and horses of all batteries taken to the Zepplin sheds on the South Eastern outskirts of MAUBEUGE. Surplus personnel sent close to R.A. Reinforcements HQ Cambrai under charge of LIEUT. MONTGOMERY. Orders received that Bde. would march to FERRIÈRE LE GRAND on the 17th. Starting at the Pontoon bridge in SOUS LE BOIS at 0945 hours.	51. 1/40. " " " " " " " " " " 51. 1/40.
		2100	Above March Order cancelled. Bde. would march via HAUTMONT, the starting point being the T roads in P.12.C. All arrangements for the 17th postponed 24 hours. At 2130 hours Staff Captain reported	
		2200		
		2130	Arrival of 56 remounts which were turned loose in B/3/2's gun park.	"WD"
SOUS LE BOIS Q.7.	17.11.18		Only 31 remounts could be found. These were exchanged for mules and indifferent horses. HQ received 1 horse. The loss of 36 head collars reported, belonging to the exchanged horses, no trace being found by 2300 hours.	51. 1/40. " " " "WD"

ORIGINAL

SHEET. 10

Army Form C. 2118.

312th Bde: R.F.A.

WAR DIARY
or
INTELLIGENCE SUMMARY.
(Erase heading not required.)

Instructions regarding War Diaries and Intelligence Summaries are contained in F. S. Regs., Part II. and the Staff Manual respectively. Title pages will be prepared in manuscript.

Place	Date	Hour	Summary of Events and Information	Remarks and references to Appendices
SOUS LE BOIS Q.7.	18.11.18.	0955	The Brigade marched to FERRIÈRE LE GRAND (A.J. NAMUR. 8.) via HAUMONT leaving the starting point, the T roads in P.12.c. at 0955, Bde. H.Q. leading followed by C, A, B, and D Batteries. Battery H.Q. baggage was brought on in rear of the Brigade. Arrived FERRIÈRE LE GRAND at 1200 hours. Over found for all personnel.	57.A/40. NAMUR. 8. 1/100.
FERRIÈRE LE GRAND. A, B, C.3.	19.11.18.	0835. 1230 1310	Brigade left FERRIÈRE LE GRAND for HANTES WIHERIES, moving via (C.3.) ROUSIES - RECQUIGNIES - ROCQ - MARPENT - JEUMONT, crossing the Belgian frontier just West of ERQUELMNES - SOLRE-SUR-SAMBRE arriving at HANTES WIHERIES at 1230 hours. The Baggage left at 0920 hours arriving at 1310 hours. Over found for all personnel. Roads muddy & heavy going. Congratulations received from Brig-General Anderson upon the turn out of the Brigade. Presentation made by the villages in the form of a song specially written for the entrance of the first troops.	NAMUR. 8. 1/100. " " " " " " NAMUR. 8. 1/100. (F.3.)
HANTES WIHERIES. C.3.	20.11.18.		Brigade marched to THY-LE-CHATEAU moving via FONTAINE HAUTE - LEERS -	

SHEET 11.   ORIGINAL

Army Form C. 2118.

372nd Bde R.F.A.

WAR DIARY
or
INTELLIGENCE SUMMARY.
(Erase heading not required.)

Instructions regarding War Diaries and Intelligence Summaries are contained in F. S. Regs, Part II. and the Staff Manual respectively. Title pages will be prepared in manuscript.

Place	Date	Hours	Summary of Events and Information	Remarks and references to Appendices
HANTES WIHERIES C.3	20.11.18	1900	LYREE – RAGNIES – THUILLIES – COUR – BERZEE to THY-LE-CHATEAU. The column arrived at dusk, the baggage being delayed by GS wagons of the Column in front did not get in until 1900 hours. The Brigade had billets on the South side of LA THYRIA river at 1900 of the Bde. H.Q. a demonstration was made to the O.C., accompanied by the village band (brass) requesting that a rest of about 5 days duration would take place here. May	NAMUR 8. 1/100 " " " " " JMP
THY-LE-CHATEAU F.3.	21.11.18		First day of frost. Batteries spent the day clearing up. Arrangements made with the villagers for two concerts for the 22nd & 23rd by the 310th Bde & 372nd Bde. Hay procured with some difficulty.	NAMUR 8. 1/100 " JMP
THY-LE-CHATEAU F.3.	22.11.18	1700 1530	Frost again. Meeting of Sports Committee held, an inter-section football Competition being arranged. A concert plus Wet Canteen, given by the 310th Bde in the Opera House finishing its tour with an open air dance. Entire members 372nd Bde. were invited.	NAMUR 8. 1/100 " " " JMP

SHEET. 12   ORIGINAL

Army Form C. 2118.

312th Bde. R.F.A.

WAR DIARY
or
INTELLIGENCE SUMMARY.
(Erase heading not required.)

Place	Date	Hour	Summary of Events and Information	Remarks and references to Appendices
THY-LE-CHATEAU. F.3.	23.11.18		First Indoor concert given by the Bde. to which certain members of the 310th Bde. were invited. Orders received that the march eastwards would be continued on the 24th. The Brigade to march to GERPINNES. (G.2.)	MANUR. 8. 1/100. " " " JMR.
THYLE-CHATEAU. F.3.	24.11.18	0905	Starting at 0908 hours the Brigade marched to GERPINNES via GOURDINNE - MANUR - SONZEE - THIRCIENNE, to SERT arriving 1120 hours. Owing to the road being very frosty the start was somewhat delayed. Having a staff discount before the starting point. Great difficulty experienced in obtaining any hay at all. Orders to march to FURNAUX (I.3.) on the 25th	MANUR. 8. 1/100. " " " " " JMR.
GERPINNEE, G.2.	25.11.18	0830	Starting at 0830 hours the Brigade marched to FURNAUX via FURNAUX HA FRONTIÉE - BIESME - SERY and METTET, arriving 1100 hours. Good hay was procured in the village. Rainy weather. Billets fair.	MANUR. 8. 1/100. " " JMR.
	1100			
FURNAUX. I.3	26.11.18	0905	At 0905 hours the Brigade left FURNAUX for MAREDRET (J.3.) marching	MANUR 1/100. JMR.

SHEET. 13
ORIGINAL

Army Form C. 2118.

WAR DIARY
or
INTELLIGENCE SUMMARY.

(Erase heading not required.)

3/2ⁿᵈ Bde. R.F.A.

Place	Date	Hour	Summary of Events and Information	Remarks and references to Appendices
FURNAUX I.3.	25.11.16	1015	HQ ERMETON, arriving 1015 hours. On the first day the surplus baggage followed the Brigade and not the Brigade Group. Food Hay procured in the village. Billets rather scattered.	NAMUR. 8. J/100 " " JNB.
MAREDRET I.3.	27.11.16	0830	Leaving MAREDRET at 0830 hours the Brigade marched via SOSOYE – FOY – PALAËN – WEILLEN – ONHAYE – DINANT – GEMMECHENNE to THYNES (L.3.). Owing to the slowness of the column in front who had pushed into the time out of turn, the Brigade was delayed	NAMUR. 8. J/100 " " " " " " "
		1545	two hours on the journey, not arriving until 1545 hours. Also billeted in the village were 30th Bde., two H.Q. & two batteries, together with the mobile V. section, making billets very crowded. Hay plentiful.	JNB.
THYNES. L.3.	28.11.16		Orders received that the Brigade would rest for several days, continuing the march on the 4th of December in all probability. No oats received in forage ration. Rain from 1100 hours.	NAMUR. 8. J/100 " JNB.

SHEET 1A. ORIGINAL

Army Form C. 2118.

3/2" Bde. R.F.A.

WAR DIARY
or
INTELLIGENCE SUMMARY.
(Erase heading not required.)

Place	Date	Hour	Summary of Events and Information	Remarks and references to Appendices
PAKES L.S.	20.11.18		All standings getting Hay hat D/312 horses lined being driven to Tally. Bitters send to inspection for Christmas dinners. Half officers shown during morning.	NAMUR 5/1/60 /MK.
PAKES L.S.	30.11.18		Still been Rohes field cashier reported to turnout. Pay day.	MK. NAMUR 8/60

R.W. Johnson Lt Col
Commanding 312 Bde RFA

Dec 2nd 1918

ORIGINAL

Army Form C. 2118.

WAR DIARY
or
~~INTELLIGENCE SUMMARY.~~

312th BRIGADE. R.F.A.

Vol 24

WAR DIARY.
DECEMBER. 1918.
312th BRIGADE. R.F.A.

VOLUME XXIV

ORIGINAL.

ORIGINAL

Army Form C. 2118.

Instructions regarding War Diaries and Intelligence
Summaries are contained in F. S. Regs., Part II.
and the Staff Manual respectively. Title pages
will be prepared in manuscript.

WAR DIARY
or
INTELLIGENCE SUMMARY.   312th BRIGADE, R.F.A.

(Erase heading not required.)

Place	Date	Hour	Summary of Events and Information	Remarks and references to Appendices
THYNES L.3	1.12.18		The whole Brigade in rest at THYNES (NAMUR 5. L.3.) Certain difficulties experienced with short rations.	NAMUR 8.1/100 " " VAS.
THYNES L.3	2.12.18		Short Rations. Orders that the Brigade would most probably march on the 7th. SP of Section B/312 & Left Section C resulted in a tie of 1 goal each	NAMUR 8.1/100 " " VAS.
THYNES L.3	3.12.18		Short Rations. Arrangements made for following the whole Brigade on the 4th & 5th	NAMUR 8.1/100 " " VAS.
THYNES L.3	4.12.18		Bread Rations no meat. 1 Section per battery to the baths at 62 D.A.C.'s H.Q. at LISOGNE (L.8.)	NAMUR 8.1/100 " " VAS.
THYNES L.3	5.12.18		1 Section per battery plus Brigade H.Q. personnel to the baths at LISOGNE.	NAMUR 8.1/100 " " VAS.
THYNES L.3	6.12.18		Orders received that the march would most probably be on the 9th the NAMUR 8.1/100 7th being cancelled. Brig. General Anderson looked round D Battery. " " Bat: H.Q. Heat Right Section D/312 by 2 goals to 1 in the intu section competition " VAS.	

ORIGINAL

Army Form C. 2118.

WAR DIARY
or
~~INTELLIGENCE SUMMARY.~~
(Erase heading not required.)

J/2 - BRIGADE, R.F.A.

Place	Date	Hours	Summary of Events and Information	Remarks and references to Appendices
THYNES. L.3	7.12.18		Orders received that the Brigade will march to the CORBION-YCHIPPE area on the 8th. Left Section A/3/2 beat Right Section C/3/2 by 1 goal to nil in the Inter Section Competition. Meeting of the 62. D.A. Football Committee. Trial by F.G.C.M. of Gnr. LEAHY of D/3/2.	NAMUR 8.1/100 MARCHE 9. " " " " " " MRS.
THYNES. L.3	8.12.18	0300	Orders received that march on 8th was cancelled until further orders. B/3/2 Left Section beat Right Section C/3/2 and again MARCHE 9. B/3/2 Left Section replayed them to settle left section tie. Kept playing extra time Capt Swain. L.C. tied with one goal all after playing extra time. had to go to hospital suffering from effects of malaria.	NAMUR. 8.1/100 MARCHE 9. " " " " " MRS.
THYNES L.3	9.12.18		Received of H.Q. under direction of Col. Johnston D.S.O. and Col. Johnston, prepared a 12 furlong steeplechase course; eight officers of the Brigade turning out for the run in the afternoon. Orders received during evening that the march arranged for the 8th would be carried out on the 10th.	NAMUR. 8.1/100 " " " " " " " " MRS.
THYNES L.3	10.12.18		Brigade marches to CORBION-YCHIPPE area (MARCHE, 9. 1/100. B.3.) Moving H.Q.	NAMUR 8.1/100 MRS.

ORIGINAL

Army Form C. 2118.

WAR DIARY
or
INTELLIGENCE SUMMARY

(Erase heading not required.)

3/2ⁿᵈ BRIGADE. R.F.A.

Instructions regarding War Diaries and Intelligence Summaries are contained in F. S. Regs., Part II. and the Staff Manual respectively. Title pages will be prepared in manuscript.

Place	Date	Hour	Summary of Events and Information	Remarks and references to Appendices
			SCRINNE and ACHENE, a distance of 9 miles arriving in the area at 1100hrs. A/3/2 and B/3/2 remained in CORBION (MARCHE.9. B.3) while HQ/3/2, C/3/2 & D/3/2 went forward to YCHIPPE (MARCHE.9.B.3) The 14th B.A.C. also being in YCHIPPE, the 325 Coy. A.S.C. being in CORBION.	MARCHE.9.1/100 " " " " " " " " " VHS.
YCHIPPE B.3.	11.12.18.	0925.	Brigade marches from CORBION-YCHIPPE and to BARVAUX CONDROZ a distance of 9½ miles having HQ CHAPOIS and PESSOUX, arriving at 1330 hours. The Brigade was delayed 50 minutes 1½ kilometres outside BARVAUX by the A.S.C. baggage being stuck on the hill the other side of the village. The four batteries are billeted in the village. Whilst HQ/3/2 found quarters in the CHATEAU CASTELLAN 1 mile S. of BARVAUX CONDROZ.	MARCHE.9.1/100 " " " " " " " " " " " " " " " " " " VHS.
BARVAUX CONDROZ	12.12.18.		Brigade marched to BARON HQ FAILON-MAPPE-MEAN-OSQUIER in forming four groups in this village were poor.	MARCHE 9. 1/100 " " " " VHS

ORIGINAL

Army Form C. 2118.

312th BRIGADE, R.F.A.

WAR DIARY
or
INTELLIGENCE SUMMARY
(Erase heading not required.)

Place	Date	Hours	Summary of Events and Information	Remarks and references to Appendices
BURNON E.2.	13.12.18		The Brigade marched to the XHORIS area (H.1) in pouring rain, hoping HQ OCQUIER-JENNERET-NEBLON-LE-PIERREUX-and HAMOIR. The area also contained the 310th Bde. R.F.A. and billeting was very close. A/312 Bty. at LES BATTYS while HQ/312 and the other three Batteries were in JEHOGNE. Billets poor. Col. M. Johnston joined th Corps from 312th Bde. as Moral Adviser to that Corps.	MARCHE 9/1/100 " " " " " " " " " " " " " " " " "
JEHOGNE H.1.	14.12.18	0920	Marching in poor weather, the Brigade left JEHOGNE at 0920 hours behind the 310th Bde. R.F.A. having H.Q. LES BATTYS-VILLE-LANDRECY-MIMIMCORD-	MARCHE 9/1/100 " "
		1320.	HOUPET and WERBOMONT. The Brigade arrived in CHEVRON at 1320 hours. HQ/312, B, C, Btys. billetted in CHEVRON, A/312 in NEUCY, D/312 in FORGES, both to the south of CHEVRON. Billets fair. 310th Bde. and 62 D. HQ also in CHEVRON. Orders that the Brigade would rest for a day.	" " " " " " "
CHEVRON Z.2	15.12.18		Spent in rest in the CHEVRON area. Orders received that the Brigade would continue the march on the 16th.	MARCHE 9/1/100

ORIGINAL

Army Form C. 2118.

Instructions regarding War Diaries and Intelligence Summaries are contained in F. S. Regs., Part II. and the Staff Manual respectively. Title pages will be prepared in manuscript.

312th BRIGADE. R.F.A

WAR DIARY
or
INTELLIGENCE SUMMARY.
(Erase heading not required.)

Place	Date	Hours	Summary of Events and Information	Remarks and references to Appendices
CHEVRON I.2.	16.12.18.		The Brigade marched to TROIS PONTS, starting at 0700 hours. Route via FORGES and BASSE BODEUX. Billets in the area were good.	MAPS 9.1/100 J.M.6.
TROIS PONTS	17.12.18		The Brigade moved to the WEISMES area, moving via STAVELOT and MALMEDY. The Head of the Brigade crossed the frontier between	MARCHE 9.1/100 " "
		1045	STAVELOT and MALMEDY, literal at 1045 hours. HQ,BD and D/312 Bde billeted in ONDENVAL (GERMANY) LV.E,3) B/312 in REMONVAL, M,BD. and C/312 Koug in THIRIMONT. Orders that the Brigade would rest in this area for two days.	" " " J.M.6.
ONDENVAL IV. E.3	18.12.18		The Brigade in Rest. Rest but weather made standing very bad.	GERMANY 1/100. J.M. J.M.6
ONDENVAL E.3	19.12.18		Brigade still in Rest. Orders that the Brigade would not move on the 20th.	" " J.M.6.
ONDENVAL E.3	20.12.18		The Rest orders cancelled. That the Brigade would march to KRYER ELSENBORN in the 21st.	" " J.M.6.

ORIGINAL

Army Form C. 2118.

WAR DIARY
or
INTELLIGENCE SUMMARY

(Erase heading not required.)

312th BRIGADE R.F.A.

Instructions regarding War Diaries and Intelligence Summaries are contained in F. S. Regs., Part II. and the Staff Manual respectively. Title pages will be prepared in manuscript.

Place	Date	Hours	Summary of Events and Information	Remarks and references to Appendices
ONDENVAL I.M. F.3	21.12.18.		The Brigade marched to LAGER EISENBORN moving via NEISMES-BÜTGENBACH GERMANY-NIDRUM. The Brigade was billetted in the German barracks. The horses of B, C, D/312 being all under cover, the billets for the men also being excellent.	I.M. 1/100. "JMS."
LAGER EISENBORN I.M. F.1	22.12.18.		The Brigade marched to HÖFEN, leaving the Artillery Group. Route via EISENBORN - KALTER HERBERG - MONTJOIE. Billets good.	I.M. 1/100 GERMANY "JMS."
HÖFEN I.L. G.11	23.12.18.		March continued to KOLLSEIFEN area. HQ/312, A,B/312, C,D/312 in MORSBACH. Route via DREIBORN. Some extremely severe rail shews were encountered on the route; the 4th her arriving not through. Orders received that the Brigade would rest on the 24th.	I.L. 1/100 " " " " "JMS."
KOLLSEIFEN I.L. I.10	24.12.18.		Brigade in rest in the KOLLSEIFEN area expecting to complete the march to the GEMÜND area on Christmas Day. Weather fine and sharp frost.	I.L. 1/100 " "JMS."

ORIGINAL

Army Form C. 2118.

Instructions regarding War Diaries and Intelligence Summaries are contained in F. S. Regs., Part II. and the Staff Manual respectively. Title pages will be prepared in manuscript.

WAR DIARY
or
INTELLIGENCE SUMMARY
(Erase heading not required.)

3rd BRIGADE R.F.A.

Place	Date	Hour	Summary of Events and Information	Remarks and references to Appendices
HOHSEIFEN I.L. I.10	25.12.18		The Brigade marched to GEMÜND via HERHAHN. Orders received that the Brigade would rest here indefinitely. 310th Bde. R.F.A. are also in GEMÜND, consequently billets were very crowded.	GERMANY. I.L. 1/100. " JMD "
GEMÜND I.L.	26.12.18.		Owing to the arrival of reinforcements to Brigade, all ranks are confined to billets yesterday & today. All Christmas dinners have been arranged for a later date, heather party 3" shoes.	" JMD "
GEMÜND I.L.	27.12.18.		Frosty. Snow still lying.	" JMD "
GEMÜND I.L.	28.12.18.		Xmas. All ranks free from the 10th [?]. Rum issue to return to unit.	" JMD "
GEMÜND I.L.	29.12.18		Snow all gone. Batch of coal miners leave the Brigade to proceed to England for demobilization.	" JMD "

233 W.W.23147454 700,000 5/15 D.D.& L. A.D.S.S./Forms/C.2118.

ORIGINAL

Army Form C. 2118.

312th BRIGADE. R.F.A.

WAR DIARY
or
~~INTELLIGENCE SUMMARY~~
(Erase heading not required.)

Instructions regarding War Diaries and Intelligence Summaries are contained in F. S. Regs., Part II. and the Staff Manual respectively. Title pages will be prepared in manuscript.

Place	Date	Hour	Summary of Events and Information	Remarks and references to Appendices
GEMOND 1.L.	30.12.18		R.A.F.E. re-established. Personnel allotted to each Brigade for constructional purposes.	GERMANY 1/10a J.M.S.
GEMOND 1.L.	31.12.18		Trench mortar personnel to join the R.A.F.E. to work as such. Inspection of all horses for C.R.A. 2nd Army ordered for 1.1.19 but later cancelled.	" J.M.S.

[signature]
Lt. Col. R.F.A.
Commanding 312th Bde. R.F.A.

Army Form C. 2118.

WAR DIARY
or
INTELLIGENCE SUMMARY.
(Erase heading not required.)

ORIGINAL COPY.

WAR DIARY.

312th Brigade. R.F.A.

JANUARY.

1919.

ORIGINAL COPY

Army Form C. 2118.

WAR DIARY
or
INTELLIGENCE SUMMARY.
(Erase heading not required.)

312th Bde. R.F.A.

Instructions regarding War Diaries and Intelligence Summaries are contained in F. S. Regs., Part II. and the Staff Manual respectively. Title pages will be prepared in manuscript.

Place	Date	Hour	Summary of Events and Information	Remarks and references to Appendices
GEMÜND.	1.1.19.		The Brigade in rest in the GEMÜND area. HQ/312, B/312 and GERMANY. 1/4. D/312 being in GEMÜND itself while A/312 were in OLEF (2 miles) 1/100,000 South of GEMÜND) C/312 in WIERFELD (1 mile South of GEMÜND).	INT "."
"	2.1.19.		Slight rain showers.	INT "."
"	3.1.19.			"
"	4.1.19.		Games of football arranged between batteries, the Brigade having won two grounds, one at GEMÜND, the other at OLEF.	INT "."
"	5.1.19.		Officers of the Brigade played the Sergeants. The game resulting in a win for the latter by 3-2. Lt-Col M.H. JOHNSON, D.S.O. handed over the Brigade on his leave to England. Major F.A. ARNOLD FORSTER, taking over the Brigade.	"
"	6.1.19.			"
"	7.1.19.		The first meeting of the Officers' French class took place under a Lt.Col. INT.	

ORIGINAL COPY

Army Form C. 2118.

Instructions regarding War Diaries and Intelligence
Summaries are contained in F. S. Regs., Part II.
and the Staff Manual respectively. Title pages
will be prepared in manuscript.

WAR DIARY
or
INTELLIGENCE SUMMARY.
(Erase heading not required.)

3/2 Bde. R.F.A.

Place	Date	Hour	Summary of Events and Information	Remarks and references to Appendices
GEMÜND	8.1.19.		Football. A/3/2. and C/3/2 drew 1-1. 'B'By beat 'D' by 3 goals to 1. The men of H.Q. Staff had their Christmas dinner.	GERMANY, 1.4. JKP 1/100.000
"	9/1/19		Sharp frost to-st night which looked like holding.	JKP
"	10/1/19		A Jena Rifle, the interpreter attached to the Brigade from the French Mission left for 3rd Army HQ, after being with the Brigade since it landed in France.	JKP
"	11.1.19.		The football match of the second round of the Section Competition resulted in a win for the Right Sec. B. v. Left Sect C. by 5-nil. 'B' Bty gave their men a dinner	JKP
"	12/1/19		HQ. played 525 Coy R.A.S.C. in the D.A. League and were beaten 3-nil. An officers match between the 3/10th Bde to be cancelled owing to snow. About 1" of snow fell in the area during the night of 11th-12th	JKP

ORIGINAL COPY.

Army Form C. 2118.

312th Bde R.F.A.

WAR DIARY
or
INTELLIGENCE SUMMARY.

(Erase heading not required.)

Instructions regarding War Diaries and Intelligence Summaries are contained in F. S. Regs., Part II. and the Staff Manual respectively. Title pages will be prepared in manuscript.

Place	Date	Hour	Summary of Events and Information	Remarks and references to Appendices
GEMÜND.	13.1.19		General Kirgour, Horse Adviser to G.H.Q. visited the Brigade and inspected the horses of D/Bty. All sores had disappeared.	GERMANY 1:100,000. J.K.R.
"	14.1.19		Slight rain in the night.	" J.K.R.
"	15.1.19		Snow in small quantity.	" J.K.R.
"	16.1.19		A/312 and C/312 horses paraded for classification by Major R. Miblets, & Capt Rowley (62 D.A.C.) B/312 and D/312 horses classified.	" J.K.R. " J.K.R.
"	17.1.19			" J.K.R.
"	18.1.19		HQ/312 and remainder of B/312 horses classified	" J.K.R.
"	19.1.19		A game of Rugby football played between two scratch sides in the Brigade.	" J.K.R.
"	20.1.19		The Brigade football ground cut for Rugby match 14.A.A.A.Bde. v. 312 Bde.	" J.K.R.

ORIGINAL COPY

Army Form C. 2118.

312th Bde. R.F.A.

WAR DIARY
or
INTELLIGENCE SUMMARY
(Erase heading not required.)

Instructions regarding War Diaries and Intelligence Summaries are contained in F.S. Regs., Part II. and the Staff Manual respectively. Title pages will be prepared in manuscript.

Place	Date	Hour	Summary of Events and Information	Remarks and references to Appendices
GEMÜND	21/1/19		Hard frost.	"JNR" GERMANY 1/4. 1/100.000
"	22/1/19		Hard frost. Ha/312 lost to A/310, D/312 lost to C/310, B/312 beat 62. Div. T.M.s. The Section Competition cancelled owing to frost.	"JNR"
"	23/1/19		Two and half inches of Snow fell during the day and last night. Captain ANDERSON. M.C. R.A.M.C. leaves the Brigade, replaced by LT. RODGERS American Medical corps.	"JNR"
"	24.			"
"	25.		Sharp frosts each night with two inches of snow on the ground made exercising and drill orders difficult.	"JNR"
"	26. 27. 28.			" " "
"	29.		A/312 changed positions with 525 Coy. R.A.S.C., moving up to SCHEVEN during the morning.	"JNR"

ORIGINAL COPY.

Army Form C. 2118.

WAR DIARY
or
INTELLIGENCE SUMMARY.

(Erase heading not required.)

3/2ⁿᵈ Bde. R.F.A.

Place	Date	Hour	Summary of Events and Information	Remarks and references to Appendices
GEMÜND	30.1.19		Brig: Gen: Anderson visited the Brigade and inspected the stables in Construction.	GERMANY 1/100,000 sheet 12.
"	31.1.19.		Slight thaw, followed by hard frost.	" "

F.A Armold-Forster Major M.F.A
Commanding 3/2 Brigade M.F.A

Army Form C. 2118.

312th Bde. R.F.A

N26

Confidential

WAR DIARY
or
~~INTELLIGENCE SUMMARY~~
(Erase heading not required.)

Summary of Events and Information

WAR DIARY

312th BRIGADE R.F.A

FEBRUARY

1919

ORIGINAL COPY

February 1919.

Instructions regarding War Diaries and Intelligence Summaries are contained in F. S. Regs., Part II. and the Staff Manual respectively. Title pages will be prepared in manuscript.

Place	Date	Hour		Remarks and references to Appendices

Army Form C. 2118.

WAR DIARY
or
INTELLIGENCE SUMMARY.
(Erase heading not required.)

Place	Date	Hour	Summary of Events and Information	Remarks and references to Appendices
GENURD	1-8.2.19		Had frost and snow limited Battery activities, to exercising only. The men found excellent amusement in tobogganing which filled most of their spare time. A certain amount of tobogganns were obtained locally.	GERMANY. 1:2. 1/100,000. JNR. JNR.
"	9.2.19		Col. R.H. Johnson. D.S.O. O.C. 3/2. Bde returned from a month leave.	JNR.
"	10-12.2.19		A New sets in and makes all standings, parks, etc. very bad.	JNR.
"	12-24.2.19		Usual training carried out, together with the recreational competition.	JNR.
"	24.2.19		Capt. F. Robinson B/3/2 BG. RFA. demobilized.	JNR.
"	27.2.19		Majr. C.R. Treay #C/3/2. Captain H.G.B. Hatcher, demobilized.	JNR.

R.H.Johnson Lt.Col. D.S.O. Bot; R.A.
O.C. 3/2. Bde. RFA 2. 3. 19.

Army Form C. 2118.

WAR DIARY
or
INTELLIGENCE SUMMARY.
(Erase heading not required.)

Confidential

ORIGINAL

MARCH
312th BRIGADE. R.F.A.
WAR DIARY
1-3-19 — "31-3-19.
VOLUME XVII

Army Form C. 2118.

WAR DIARY
or
INTELLIGENCE SUMMARY.
(Erase heading not required.)

312th Bde. R.F.A.

Place	Date	Hour	Summary of Events and Information	Remarks and references to Appendices
GEMÜND GERMANY.	1-31		Throughout the month the Brigade remained in the GEMÜND area, HQ B/312, B/312, and D/312 in the village of GEMÜND, A/312 at SCHEVEN, and C/312 at MERFELD. During the month no happenings of military importance took place. During the month two officers and 14 N.C.O.s and other ranks were demobilized, while during the same period the Brigade received drafts of 1 officer, 64 N.C.O.s and other ranks. Little having been carried out during the month while during spare time, recreational competitions were organised with success for all ranks. Three officers were transferred to England for duty in India.	GERMANY 1:L. 1/100,000 Appx. Appx. Appx. Appx.

R M Sweeny
Lieut Colonel, R.F.A.
O.C. 312th Brigade R.F.A.

WAR DIARY
or
INTELLIGENCE SUMMARY.

Army Form C. 2118.

WAR DIARY
312th Bde. R.F.A
MAY
1919

Army Form C.2118.

WAR DIARY
or
INTELLIGENCE SUMMARY.
(Erase heading not required.)

Instructions regarding War Diaries and Intelligence Summaries are contained in F. S. Regs., Part II. and the Staff Manual respectively. Title pages will be prepared in manuscript.

Place	Date	Hour	Summary of Events and Information	Remarks and references to Appendices
GEMUND				GERMANY
	MAY		Lt Col Patterson Barker assumed the duties of O.C. Brigade During the month 9 Officers and 101 other ranks were posted to the Brigade while 1 officer and 81 men were demobilized Two (2) officers were also posted away	1/10000
			A Battery reamoured from SCHEVEN and stationed at GEMUND while 'C' Battery was shifted from NIERFELD to NAHSBENDEN	
			A table of Battery & Section training was commenced	MPN

C Morris
Lt Col RA
OC 312 Bde RFA

Army Form C. 2118.

312 BRIGADE R.F.A.

WAR DIARY
or
INTELLIGENCE SUMMARY.
(Erase heading not required.)

WAR DIARY

312th Bde - R.F.A.

JUNE

1919

Army Form C. 2118.

WAR DIARY
or
INTELLIGENCE SUMMARY.
(Erase heading not required.)

Place	Date	Hour	Summary of Events and Information	Remarks and references to Appendices
GEMUND GERMANY	JUNE		Major C.E.F. GAITSKILL (T.F.) R.F.A. assumed command of C/312 vice Major F.A. ARNOLD	1/1/0000
			FORSTER (T.F.) R.F.A. demobilized.	
			During the month two officers were demobilized and nine were posted away.	
			Battery training was commenced.	
	June 12th		The Brigade was inspected by the Commander-in-Chief General Sir W.R. Robertson G.C.B. K.C.V.O. D.S.O. A.D.C. at NIERFELD. The Brigade was in Drill Order (Mounted) with Steel helmets. The Band of the 51st Gordon Highlanders was on parade. The C-in-C. expressed great satisfaction.	

C Davim
Lt Col
Commdg
312 B. R.F.A

ORIGINAL

Army Form C. 2118.

WAR DIARY
or
INTELLIGENCE SUMMARY. 312 Bde. R.F.A.
(Erase heading not required.)

Instructions regarding War Diaries and Intelligence Summaries are contained in F. S. Regs., Part II. and the Staff Manual respectively. Title pages will be prepared in manuscript.

WAR DIARY.
312th Bde. R.F.A.

JULY 1919.

(Unknown)

Place	Date	Hour	Summary of Events and Information	Remarks and references to Appendices

WAR DIARY
or
INTELLIGENCE SUMMARY. 312th Bde. R.F.A.

Army Form C. 2118.

Place	Date	Hour	Summary of Events and Information	Remarks and references to Appendices
GEMUND	JULY		On the 10th July C/312 proceed under command of Major R. Horfall to ESSENBORN range they carried out the 15th carrying out firing practice. During the week 2 officers and 1 O.R. were demobilized, while 2 officers and 6 men joined the Brigade. Nothing else to report.	

J.B.19

(Sd) H. Col. R.A.
Commanding 312 Bde R.F.A.

Army Form C. 2118.

Regimental 62 Div.
3/2 Bde. R.F.A.

ORIGINAL

WAR DIARY
or
INTELLIGENCE SUMMARY.
(Erase heading not required.)

Instructions regarding War Diaries and Intelligence Summaries are contained in F. S. Regs., Part II. and the Staff Manual respectively. Title pages will be prepared in manuscript.

Place	Date	Hour	Summary of Events and Information	Remarks and references to Appendices
			3/2 BRIGADE R.F.A WAR DIARY AUGUST. 1919.	

Army Form C. 2118.

WAR DIARY
or
INTELLIGENCE SUMMARY.   312 Bde. R.F.A.

(Erase heading not required.)

Place	Date	Hour	Summary of Events and Information	Remarks and references to Appendices
	1.8.19 – 16.8.19		The Brigade stationed at GEMUND, GERMANY.	
GEMUND GERMANY			The Brigade held a very Successful Horse Show on the 4th Aug: but the same night received orders to commence dispersing with the animals. By 10.8.19 all animals and vehicles were despatched to England while the Brigade entrained at GEMUND STATION on the 13th for DUREN. The next night was spent in DUREN Barracks, & that of the 14/15/= spent in the train en route to CALAIS. The Brigade left calais on the 16th for DOVER arriving CODFORD Station at 1 a.m on the 17th.	J.M.L.
HEYTESBURY CAMP YORKSHIRE	17.8.19 – 31.8.19		Since its arrival in England all Ranks have been granted 14 days leave. Batteries in possession of no vehicles & 50 horses per unit. The Brigade demobilized H.Q, N.C.Os + ORs and received nil. Nothing else of importance to record. J.M. Whitworth ?/Adjt; 312 Bde. R.F.A. ?/Lt. O.C.	J.M.L.

www.ingramcontent.com/pod-product-compliance
Lightning Source LLC
Chambersburg PA
CBHW081406160426
43193CB00013B/2117